THE WARRIOR WHO KILLED CUSTER

The Warrior
Who Killed Custer

The Personal Narrative of
Chief Joseph White Bull

Translated and edited by
JAMES H. HOWARD

UNIVERSITY OF NEBRASKA PRESS · LINCOLN

970.3092
D135ω
1968

Publishers on the Plains
UNP

Foreword

CHIEF JOSEPH WHITE BULL, or Pte-san-hunka, was one of the foremost Teton Dakota (Western Sioux) warriors during the most critical period in that group's history. The son of the Miniconjou chief Makes-room, and the nephew of the famous Sitting Bull of the Hunkpapas, White Bull, born in 1850, was trained from infancy for warfare and the hunt. As he grew to maturity he played a major role in the bitter struggle of the Tetons to protect their hunting grounds against the advancing white frontier. In his later years White Bull was made a chief himself. The subject of a biographical account by Stanley Vestal, White Bull was later advanced by Vestal as the warrior who slew, in personal combat, General George A. Custer.[1]

In 1931, many years after he had fought his last battle and killed his last buffalo, White Bull was persuaded to describe the colorful events of his past life. Writing in his native Dakota tongue and using the traditional pictographs of his people to further amplify his account, White Bull produced the remarkable document which is reproduced and translated in this volume. Included are descriptions of various hunts and battles in which White Bull participated, including three views of White Bull killing Custer. Also included is one of the traditional winter counts, or calendrical histories, of the Dakotas, providing a record of the Tetons from 1764/65 through 1930/31. This winter count, however, is not accompanied by pictographs.

[1] Stanley Vestal, *Warpath: The True Story of the Fighting Sioux Told in a Biography of Chief White Bull* (Boston: Houghton Mifflin Co., 1934); "The Man Who Killed Custer," *American Heritage*, Vol. VIII, No. 2 (1957), pp. 4–9, 90–91.

The entire account, written and drawn in an old-fashioned business ledger, was purchased from White Bull by Mr. Usher L. Burdick of Fargo, North Dakota. In 1959 the manuscript was purchased from Mr. Burdick by the Chester Fritz Library of the University of North Dakota, where it remains in the Orrin G. Libby Manuscript Collection. During the summer of 1960, assisted by a grant from the University of North Dakota research fund, I was able to secure a complete translation of the manuscript, plus interpretations of some of the symbolic details of the pictographs. Of particular assistance in this project were Mr. and Mrs. Bennett Sierra, Teton Dakotas of Pine Ridge, South Dakota, and Mr. Stephen E. Feraca, then employed by the Indian Service at Pine Ridge. Miss Ella Deloria, a Yankton Dakota anthropologist whose special field is the Dakota language, also provided welcome assistance later in the project.

In the interest of accuracy, I have retained White Bull's original orthography in reproducing the Dakota text. Most of those reading this book will not be familiar with the Dakota language. Those who are can easily supply the accent marks, nasalizations, etc., currently employed by the linguist in transcribing Dakota speech. The alphabet used by White Bull is that developed for Dakota by the missionary Stephen R. Riggs. It is an earlier form, however, than that used by Riggs in his *Dakota-English Dictionary* of 1890. White Bull's written Dakota is excellent in style, the only idiosyncrasy being his tendency to indicate plurality in nouns, a custom not followed by most Dakotas. My translation, as one will quickly note, is quite free. I have endeavored, however, to capture the exact meaning and flavor of the original. Editorial insertions in White Bull's text are bracketed.

In numbering the pages of the White Bull manuscript, I have treated White Bull's letter of transmittal to Mr. Burdick as page one, then numbered each page in the ledger which contains any written or pictorial material in succession from two through fifty-one. There are thirty-three blank pages in the

ledger between pages eight and nine, and forty-eight more at
the back of the book following the page I have numbered
fifty-one. Generally, White Bull has written and drawn his
pictographs only on the right-hand pages of the ledger. Pages
two, three, and forty-eight, however, are on the left-hand
side. In all instances but one the pictographs are oriented so
that the bottom of the pictograph is toward the stitching of
the ledger. The written material in the manuscript is in ink.
Where there is a considerable amount of text White Bull has
generally lined the pages of the ledger with a pencil and
straightedge.

The pictographs are done in a combination of ink, lead
pencil, and colored crayon. The lead pencil is generally used
to indicate black or dark brown (such as the tips of eagle
feathers) or dark blue (such as the navy-blue color of trade
cloth). Ink is generally used to outline figures, though occasionally lead pencil is used for this as well. White Bull's pictographs show careful attention to costume detail and a lively
sense of action. Although his work would probably not be
rated among the best in Teton art of this period, it is good.

JAMES H. HOWARD

Contents

ix

List of Plates

Black and white plates following page 74:

Introduction

SINCE THE WHITE BULL NARRATIVE was produced by a member of the Teton division of the Dakota, or Sioux, tribe, and since it reflects the ethos of that people, a few words about Teton culture and history may help the reader understand more fully the events depicted and described in the manuscript and the way of life it represents.

Though first known in what is now north-central Minnesota in 1679, the Teton division of the Dakotas shortly afterward began a movement west. The De L'Isle map of 1701 shows them around the present Lake Traverse, on the Minnesota–South Dakota border, and by 1750 some groups were well established on the Missouri River and had begun ranging beyond it in their quest for the buffalo. Ultimately the High Plains country of what is now trans-Missouri North and South Dakota, with adjacent portions of western Nebraska, north-eastern Colorado, eastern Wyoming, and eastern Montana, came to be regarded as the Teton domain.

Today the Tetons are undoubtedly the best known of all the Dakotas. Originally, however, in their woodland home, the Tetons were merely one of seven bands, or council fires, making up the Dakota nation. Even today hazy accounts persist of a time when all seven groups gathered once a year to settle tribal affairs. The original seven bands, or fires, were the Mdewakantons, or "Spirit Lake people," the Wahpekutes, or "shooters among the leaves," the Sissetons, whose name is of unclear derivation but is said to refer to ridges of scales left after cleaning fish, and the Wahpetons, or "dwellers among the leaves," who, along with the first three bands named, are commonly known as the Santee, or Eastern, Dakotas; the Yanktons, or "dwellers at the end (of the camping circle)," and the Yanktonais, or "little dwellers at the end (of the camping circle)," who together are sometimes termed the middle Dakotas, or *Wičiyela*, meaning "they speak like men"; and the Tetons, or "plains dwellers."

It can be inferred from this arrangement that originally the Teton, or western, band of the Dakotas was not much larger, numerically, than any of the other six bands. Following their migration onto the High Plains, however, this single band became larger in population than all of the other six combined. Therefore, in the case of the Tetons, it is important to note the various subbands. As in the case of the Dakota tribe as a whole, the Teton subdivisions are seven in number, seven being a holy number to the Dakotas. These subbands are the Hunkpapa, or "campers at the horn or end of the camp circle"; the *Mnikondžu*, or Miniconjou or *Hohwodžu*, meaning "planters beside the water"; the *Sihasapa*, or Blackfoot (not to be confused with the Algonquian-speaking Blackfoot tribe); the *Itazipčo*, or Sans Arcs, meaning "those without bows"; the *Oohenonpa*, or Two Kettles; the *Sičangu*, or Brulé, meaning "burnt thighs"; and the Oglalas, or "those who scatter their own." Of these seven, the Brulé and Oglala were the largest subbands, and occupied a southerly position in respect to the other five.

It would appear that the change by the Tetons from a mixed horticultural-hunting prairie economy to the nomadic-hunting High Plains way of life came about gradually and in a somewhat haphazard fashion. The story of how one Teton band, the Oglalas, crossed the Missouri to become bison-hunting nomads has been preserved in a legend told to anthropologist Ella Deloria by an old Oglala man named Left-hand. It seems that a band of Tetons were traveling where a creek (the present Platte Creek, in Charles Mix and Aurora counties, South Dakota) enters the Missouri. They had no horses at the time, and were starving because of a shortage of meat. There were about thirty or forty tipis in the camp (they were very small in those days, as the tribe had no pack animals but dogs).

The camp crier called the men to go after buffalo, which had been seen on the frozen Missouri. The hunters found the herd and chased them far out on the ice, where the buffaloes' hooves could not hold, so the Indians were able to get close to them, and killed many. Since they happened to be nearer the west bank of the river after the slaughter, they dragged the hides and meat to that side and made camp to finish preparing the meat and robes. They intended to return to the east side of the river, but before they could do so a warm chinook melted the ice and left them stranded on the unfamiliar west bank. Gradually, as spring came, they moved up from the valley of the Missouri to the uplands.

They continued traveling around on the west side of the Missouri. One day the scouts saw two strange objects in the distance. As they came closer it appeared to be two men riding strange giant dogs (horses). The men were friendly but spoke a language unintelligible to the Dakotas. Finally they drew signs on the ground indicating that the Dakotas should follow them, and in two days they would come up with the main camp of their people. These men were Cheyenne scouts.

The Dakota band followed the two men and in two days came to the camp. It was in the valley of the White River, and was the largest camp the Tetons had ever seen. The lodges were very big—since the Cheyennes had horses to drag the poles—and large horse herds grazed in the adjoining pastures. The Cheyennes treated the Dakotas royally, and at the end of their visit they gave the Teton headmen horses. Finally they left, but ever since that meeting the Dakotas have been friends of the Cheyennes and their allies, the Arapahos. From this event the Dakotas named Platte Creek *Pte kdi inyanka*, meaning "buffalo returned running," and remember it as the place where the Oglalas crossed the frozen Missouri.

The foregoing story, although undoubtedly altered and simplified in the manner of all oral traditions, probably represents a fairly accurate account of the sort of happening which led the various Teton subbands to cross the Missouri.

Subsequently, as their numbers increased, the Tetons ranged southward into Nebraska, westward into Colorado and Wyoming, and northward into western North Dakota and Montana, with occasional forays into western Manitoba and eastern Saskatchewan. Bitterly resisting the incursions of the whites, they acquired a notoriety and, when warfare had ended, fame. Today they have come to be considered the Plains Indian par excellence, and from them have come most of the popular ideas about the Dakotas, and indeed, about Indians in general.

Once the Tetons had moved onto the High Plains, bison was the mainstay of their economy, supplemented by deer and pronghorn antelope flesh. The various subbands traveled widely following the herds, and in fact it was rare for more than one or two of the subbands to camp together, except at the Sun Dance, for this reason. The steady diet of bison meat was varied with *tipsina* (*Psoralea esculenta*) and other wild foods gathered by the women. Occasionally women planted corn and other vegetables in small gardens, but more often such foods were secured by raiding or by trading with the Arikaras, the Pawnees, the Poncas, and other horticulturalists. Fish were despised as unclean food.

The tipi was the principal dwelling of the Tetons, and some tipis were large enough to permit dancing inside. Now and then a hide-covered wikiup was built as a temporary dwelling, and several of the Teton winter counts mention that the Sans Arcs built and lived in earth lodges in the winters of 1815/16 and 1816/17. The easily dismantled and readily portable tipi remained the principal dwelling for the Tetons, however, both in summer and in winter.

Teton household equipment, like that of other High Plains groups, was durable and made in such a way that it could be easily packed and transported. For carrying dried meat and larger items of clothing, a decorated parfleche made of a single piece of rawhide folded into an envelope shape was used. Cylindrical parfleches were used for warbonnets, and smaller pouches of rawhide or tanned skin were used for personal belongings and medicines. Even the elaborate double-trailed warbonnets and the "crow belts," or dancing bustles, were designed so that they could be rolled up or dismantled and packed into a small space when the camp was on the move.

Cooking utensils were as light and durable as the other articles of Teton equipment. Since pottery vessels were unsuitable for a nomadic way of life, their use was abandoned by the Tetons once they moved onto the Plains. Instead they used skin containers and frequently cooked their food by the "stone boiling" method, boiling their food by adding hot stones to a paunch containing water and raw meat, and replacing the hot stones when they became cooled. Later, after the Tetons secured metal kettles, this ancient method of cookery was used only by men on war parties who had not brought a kettle with them. Bowls were sometimes made by carving out a burl from an elm or box elder tree, and spoons were made of bison horn.

The characteristic local group of the Tetons was the *tiošpaye*, or camp. These *tiošpaye* were essentially bilateral and bilocal kin groups. Each was headed by one or more chiefs. A number of such *tiošpaye* together made up one of the seven subbands of the Tetons. Membership in both the *tiošpaye* and the subband was rather fluid, and families could join or withdraw from a group as they chose. While camping with a particular *tiošpaye* or subband, however, a family was subject to all of its rules and regulations.

From early accounts, one gathers that most Teton chiefs were largely self-made, though informants have stated that on some occasions chiefs were selected by a council of all the adult males in the subband, and that chieftainship tended to be hereditary in certain families. However chosen, it is certain that once a man had attained the office it was largely his personal qualities and success in leading the group in war and in the hunt that determined the size of his following, since people were free to leave the camp of an unpopular man.

Although details of organization differed from subband to subband, the council and chiefs emerge as the principal governing body. Some subbands, such as the Oglalas, are said to have elected four "shirt-wearers," or supreme councilors, who, though not chiefs themselves, sat with the chiefs and council and wielded authority comparable to that of the chiefs. The famous Crazy Horse, though often termed a chief, was actually one of these shirt-wearers. The orders of the chiefs, council, and shirt-wearers were carried out by four *wakičun*, or head councilors, who were assisted by two head *akičita*, or "soldiers," and a larger "soldier," or police, group of lower rank. Among the Tetons it was customary to select an entire warrior society for police, or "soldier," duty.

Theoretically, the council acted as a balance to the power of the chiefs, but in actuality, particularly during the period of the Indian Wars, many chiefs came to possess almost dictatorial power. This was particularly true in the case of men such as Sitting Bull and Red Cloud, who often paid little heed to the words of the council.

Among the Tetons, warfare and the hunt were all-important male activities, and the women were proud to share in the reflected glory of sons, brothers, and husbands. There was an elaborate system of age-graded warrior societies, each of which had its own customs, songs, dances, and costumes. Often an intense rivalry developed between certain pairs of societies, and the group which had gained the more honors on a recent raid might "steal" the wives of their rivals temporarily.

From the time the Tetons entered the High Plains region until the closing decades of the nineteenth century they were rich in horses, buffalo robes, and trade goods. They had a tremendous *esprit de corps* and a flair for doing things in the grand manner. Poorer groups, such as the Middle Dakotas and the Santees, were scorned by the Tetons, who often showed their contempt by bestowing costly gifts on their less well-to-do tribesmen. Clearly, Teton culture of the nineteenth century was a burgeoning thing, and it was during the heyday of the Tetons that Joseph White Bull lived the greater part of his life, recorded in the pages that follow.

The Warrior Who Killed Custer

PAGE 1   LETTER OF TRANSMITTAL

August 31, 1931

   Mita kola August 25 1931 Anpetu kin len wowapi wan miyeca
ran ca iwacu welo mazaska kin tanyan iwacu welo kola na on ma
ki le micu wo ehelo ho wana ecel ecamon welo hehanl taku eheci
hecetu welo tka miṡ lecel epi kte lo wowapi oowa okicize owicořan
mitawa ki lena tona wanlake ci henaecerci owa ma ya ṡi ca iyena
ke ca eceřci owawa yelo nakun [four letters crossed out] lakota
omaka ya wapi wan yacin kin ecel owawayelo ho hena on wikcemna zaptan maya qu kta ke helo he hecetu welo. Tka e e nakun
isanm ake etan han el awakamna kta wacin na etanhan el awakamna
kta wacin na etan han ota rci el koya el owowayelo ca wana
wanlake lo kola owicořan lena e e ṡunkakan okupi owapi kin lena
e e nakun [crude drawing of a tipi] tipi lakota tipi lena e e nakun
nakun makawitaki le Ṙe sapa ki le el taku ota kin e e iyapi ota rci
owicořan ota rci nakun miye el ite omiciwa lena wake ci e e yelo
tka lena on otuyařci el wowapi ota wakarelo kola [second page
of letter] hena nakes wanlake lo ho hecetu welo he on kola el
tanyan oyable ze kte lo tanyan ilukcan kta wacin yelo oowa kin
hena inṡ eya tokel ikipi ilukcan na he on i unṡimalayo kola owotanla ociciyake lo kola wicaṡa ksapa hen řca owotanla hen řca
wicaṡa waṡte henica ki he an wo owotanla okna icante waṡtepi wo
ecun okare okna oecun owotanla woknaye wanilya ociciyakelo
kola ho amayupta wo kola wana cante waṡte ya niye nakun napeci-
yuzelo nitakuyepi nakun napewicabluzelo nitakolapi wan miye
                    JOSEPH CHIEF WHITE BULL
                    PTE SAN HUNKA

   Ohokam kola wowapi ki ocici wa ki he hecel tu we wanji cin
hu wo epelo kola owotan la wacin na miye lakota iyapi okna
wowapi ki le miye wakaře lo hecel iyo nicipi hu wo kola henala
epelo

August 31, 1931

   MY FRIEND: Today, August 25, 1931, I received the letter which
you wrote me and also the money. Friend, you have asked me to

send [return] something and I have done as you wished. What you say is so, but I would like to say this. My war record, as I have written it, is accurate and I have written it for you. You said you would give me fifty dollars for it and that is all right, but I would like to earn more, and as you see I have written much more. Friend, this is the record, the record of the time they took [brought] the horses and the tipis of the Dakota. There was much talk about this when I was out in our land, the Black Hills, that time. There were lots of speeches and there was a lot going on, and I had my picture taken. That is what I mean. But I have written all this without payment, friend, as you see. That is all right. So friend, I want you to look well into this, and think it over carefully. You can give me what you think is right for the record, friend. I have told you the truth friend. You are a wise man and a fair one, and that is why you will be pleased to have it right. The record is correct and without untruths as I have told you friend. Answer me, friend. I am happy to shake your hand and also that of your relations. I remain,

> JOSEPH, CHIEF WHITE BULL
> PTE SAN HUNKA

Later, friend, someone else may want the record I wrote for you, and if so, let me hear from you, friend. I want it right and that is why I have written this in Dakota myself as I know you will be pleased, friend. That is all I will say.

This letter was undoubtedly written to Usher L. Burdick by White Bull upon receipt of Burdick's check for White Bull's work. Stapled to the original is Burdick's check for fifty dollars, made out to "Chief White Bull" and drawn on the Fargo National Bank, Fargo, North Dakota. The check is noted as being in payment for a "Sioux History Book." It is dated 8/26/1931, and is not canceled.

PAGE 2   BUFFALO HUNTING

Hektam waniyetu lena makeca el 31 years hehan Pahazizipa el Pteïcaka otapi miye kinyan ka wakli etan owapa 5 zaptan owapa

na wanase a i wana Buhiklapi na miś wana tokeya i wa hun ni
yelo Pte ki ll ake wanji wicawaowelo hecela henakeca wicawao-
wela nakan waniyetu ca lila waśme lo hanhepi ca wakli onkupelo
hanhepi mazaśkaśka 9 napcinyunka wocetu el Pte eya wicawakuwa
na wanji waowelo yunkan lila cepala rca ke lo okise yelo wapata na
waona wahina wakli wakli na hihan na el kli yo wa i tasake śni
tanye kel wawopa te lo ataye rci awakli ye lo inumpa can el ake
wanase a i ca ake tokeya iwahumni yelo hel 7 śakowin wicawaowelo
ake wanase a i ca hel 2 blala waowelo hel talo qi kte ci wanjila o wa
i nahe on ibloketu el ake wanase a i ca el hehan wanayetu [*sic*] lena
makeca 34 years el Ptehincala wan hi sapa ca kayak wa yelo blu on
kin apawarte lo he akli pelo waśican [*sic*] wan Dupree eciyapi nakan
cankajipa eciyapi ca lakota winyan wan yuza ca he waqu we lo hetan
śunke ca akan na a ke lo he an etan ota icara pelo winyela ki he an
ota isam kicitonpelo ota wanase a i ye lo tka eyaś ita he hecetu kte
lo kola

PTE SAN HUNKA
CHIEF WHITE BULL

[A badly overexposed and faded snapshot of Chief White Bull
dressed in buckskins and warbonnet and carrying his lance and
pipe is pasted to the bottom of this page.]

Many years back, when I was thirty-one years old, I went hunting near Slim Butte.[1] I brought back many buffalo[2] that time. Five
other men were hunting with me on that occasion. When we saw
the herd we all charged and I got up to them first. I shot eleven
cows on that occasion.[3] It was in the wintertime and the snow was
very deep. By the time we had skinned and dressed our meat it
was already dark, about 9 P.M.

[1] Slim Butte is a prominent geographical feature in the southwestern
part of Shannon County, South Dakota. Many of the events recounted
here are also described in Stanley Vestal's *Warpath: The True Story of the
Fighting Sioux Told in a Biography of Chief White Bull* (Boston: Houghton
Mifflin, 1934), pp. 238–239.
[2] The Dakota text translates literally as "real cows." The more common
word for bison is *tatanka*.
[3] Plains Indian buffalo hunters generally sought out the cows in a herd,
as their meat was tenderer than that of the bulls.

As we were coming back we saw another group of buffalo. I charged them and succeeded in killing one. It was a very fat cow. I skinned it about halfway and then the light was gone. The next morning I went after it. The meat wasn't frozen and I got it. I took my time and did it right, butchering the whole animal.

The second day after this I went hunting again. Once more I was the first to reach the herd when we charged. This time I killed seven. We hunted in that area one more time that winter and on the last hunt I secured only two. The meat made a heavy load for my pony.

I remember a summer hunt when I was thirty-four years old. On that hunt I saw a buffalo calf with black horns. I roped him with my lariat, threw him down, and tied his feet together. I had heard that a white man named Dupree was looking for a buffalo calf so I took it to him. This man was called "Whittler" by the Dakotas. He had taken a Dakota woman as his wife. I took the buffalo calf to him. He gave me a fine horse in return, which I rode back to the village. He raised a whole herd of buffalo from that calf, which was a female, at his place on Bad River.

I went on many buffalo hunts after that, but I remember these two best of all, friend.

PTE SAN HUNKA
CHIEF WHITE BULL

PAGE 3   WHITE BULL'S GENEALOGY

Wo o kla ke le e yelo Chief White Bull woklakelo wicarcalapi kin le omaka yawapi heca yelo [a small drawing of a human hand pointing to the right, done in ink and colored with a brown wax crayon, appears at this point] lena Pte san hunka lena iye rca miye owawayelo kola tona le wowapi kin hena oyasin epelo waniyetu lena makeca yelo wana 81 years 1931 August 9. Anpetu kin le o wa i wacu welo kola

Chief White Bull Pte san hunka miye yelo kolapi la Kinyukanpi W.B. ate wayelo mnikowoju wicaśa itancan heca tatankinyotake lekśi wayelo

wiyaka waśte win ina wayelo

tatanka wanjila sanka wayelo kola hecetu
   Wiyaka waste win sankaku kin le eyelo
tatankinyotake e tatanka psica—tawicu kin le a [anpetu okicamna
win] lena cinca pelo l owanjila pelo atkuku. hunku. owanjipila
yelo na mis eya. misunkala tatanka wanjila. kici ate ena ina kici
omawanjila yelo kolapila oyate oyasin slonya pelo kola wowicake
ece ociciyakelo kola.

   This is my statement. I, Chief White Bull, say this: I am now an
old man and have lived through many seasons, and I speak thus
[a small drawing of a human hand pointing to the right, done in
ink and colored with a brown wax crayon, appears at this point]:
This I, Chief White Bull himself, have written my friend. Everything that is in this book, all of it, I said. This year I am eighty-one
years old, as of August 9, 1931. I received it on this day, friend.
   I am Chief White Bull, Pte san hunka, my friends. My father
was Makes-room White Bull, a Miniconjou chief. Sitting Bull was
my uncle. Good-feather-woman is my mother. One Bull is my
younger brother. It is so, my friend.
   Good-feather-woman was the younger sister of Sitting Bull,
and Jumping-bull was his wife. [Whirling-day-woman] was their
child.
   We are all of one family, the father, mother, and myself and my
younger brother, One Bull. We have the same father and mother
and are of the same family. My friends, all the tribe know this is
the truth which I am telling you, friends.

PAGES 4–8   WHITE BULL'S WINTER COUNT

   Included in White Bull's personal history is a typical Teton
Dakota winter count, or calendrical history. The count is a
slightly different version of the one which White Bull supplied
to Stanley Vestal, and which Vestal included as an appendix
to his biography of White Bull, *Warpath: The True Story of the
Fighting Sioux, Told in a Biography of Chief White Bull*. Vestal
states (p. 259) that White Bull became a "keeper of the count"
when he was twenty-nine years old. He secured his count

from Hairy-hand, a Miniconjou, who had acquired it from his (Hairy-hand's) brother-in-law, a wise old man named Steamboat, or Fire-boat. White Bull purchased the calendar, then called in a number of old Teton historians to discuss it with them and thus familiarize himself with the various events.

When he secured the winter count from Hairy-hand it was in the form of a hide with pictographs painted, in a sunwise spiral, to mark off the various winters, or years. (According to the Dakotas, each year, or winter, began in the spring and ended with the following winter's termination.) The pictographs were used as mnemonic aids by the keeper of the count, who memorized an explanatory phrase for each one. But, as Vestal notes: "Having learned to write in his own language, White Bull saw no need to rely upon painted hides for his chronology, and transcribed the events of each year in a book purchased for that purpose" (p. 259).

Vestal—and apparently White Bull as well—believed that White Bull's count began with the event for 1781. A comparison of the two White Bull counts with other Teton winter counts, however, reveals that the actual beginning date is 1764/65. In the version presented here there is a hiatus from 1816/17 to 1835/36, when the count takes up again. The count ends with the year 1930/31. It is interesting to note that in the present version of his count (though not in the one published by Vestal) White Bull omits the famous meteoric shower of 1833, an event included in every other Plains Indian winter count. Of the following material, only the Dakota text was provided by White Bull.

Page 4

1. [1764/65] *Pte anuwan pelo.* "They swim towards buffalo."

This may be the same event given by Battiste Good for the year 1771/72.[4] Vestal gives it for 1781 (p. 259). Most of the

---

[4] Garrick Mallery, *Picture Writing of the American Indians*, Tenth Annual Report of the Bureau of American Ethnology, 1888–1889 (Washington, 1893), p. 306.

tribes living along the Missouri secured a part of their yearly meat supply by swimming out and towing ashore buffalo that had attempted to cross on the weak ice the previous winter and which were floating past the village.

2. [1765/66] *Toka mila yuke lo.* "When we first had knives."

This year's event refers to the first steel knives acquired by the Tetons from Europeans. According to Vestal, these knives were secured from an English trader (p. 259).

3. [1766/67] *Tajuškala ciye ku te lo.* "Little-ant's elder brother died."

4. [1767/68] *Walerola ti kte pelo.* "Little-paunch was murdered."

Vestal translates this man's name as Pemmican-bag (p. 260).

5. [1768/69] *Wazikute wayaka yuza pelo.* "Shoots-pine was taken captive."

6. [1769/70] *Iyeska kicizapelo.* "Interpreters [?] fought one another."

Vestal gives the translation "People Speaking the Same Language Quarreled" and explains that this year's event refers to a feud within the tribe (p. 260). Today the word *Iyeska* (literally, "white" or "clear speaker") is used to refer to interpreters, and by extension, to all mixed-bloods, as they often served in that capacity.

7. [1770/71] *Anunk omiye pelo.* "Attacked the camp from both sides."

Battiste Good gives this event, or a similar one, for 1769/70 and explains that a mounted war party, the tribe unknown, attacked the village from both sides, and on each side killed a woman.[5] Vestal, on the other hand, states that it was a continuation of the previous year's intratribal feud (p. 260).

8. [1771/72] *Ite haki ton la te lo.* "Wears-a-mask died."

9. [1772/73] *Wakan sica wan bleze sni.* "A bad god went berserk."

[5] *Ibid.*

Vestal states that this year's event refers to a man who claimed to be a shaman, continually spoke of his supernatural powers, and eventually lost his mind (p. 260).

10. [1773/74] *Miwatani ti ile wicayayapi.* "They burned the Mandan lodges."

11. [1774/75] *Canqi i yamni ahi wicaktepi.* "They killed three who went after wood."

Vestal explains that three women were killed by a Crow war party while gathering firewood near the village (p. 260).

12. [1775/76] *Ho ke kaŕa ta.*

The Dakota text is unclear. Perhaps *Ho ke* is a corrupted form of *Heyoka*, in which case the text might be translated as "Plays-the-clown died." Vestal gives "Made-Himself-Like-the-Man-in-the-Moon Died" (p. 260).

13. [1776/77] *Paha ta i wan ahiktepi.* "They killed a man who went on a hill."

The man referred to in this year's event apparently was scouting from a hilltop or else performing the *hambleciya*, or rite of the vigil. Vestal states that the event occurred east of the Missouri and that the man was a Miniconjou killed by the Crows (p. 260).

14. [1777/78] *Oglala ki ŕante wan icupi.* "The Oglalas brought back a cedar tree."

This year's event allegedly refers to the discovery of the Black Hills by the Dakotas, who brought back a cedar tree of a new species to verify their discovery.[6] The man who brought back the tree was named Standing-bull.

15. [1778/79] *Waniti sni awetu pelo.* "Winter camp in no particular place."

This year, probably because of mild weather, the Tetons did not establish a permanent winter camp, but continued to

---

[6] Garrick Mallery, *Pictographs of the North American Indians,* Fourth Annual Report of the Bureau of American Ethnology, 1882–1883 (Washington, 1886), p. 130.

move camp from time to time. Battiste Good gives this event for 1777/78.[7]

16. [1779/80] *Slukela ȟaki wata yapi.*

The Dakota text is unclear, but this is probably the same event given by Battiste Good for the year 1778/79. The explanation is "Skinned-penis used in the game of *Haka* winter." A Dakota named "Skinned-penis" (i.e., circumcised) was killed by the Pawnees. His Dakota companions hid the body, but the Pawnees found it and used it as a gaming stick in their game of *Haka*, which is a form of hoop-and-pole.[8]

17. [1780/81] *Cannaksa yuha ahiktepi.* "They came and killed 'Has-a-warclub.'"

Battiste Good gives this event for 1776/77.[9]

18. [1781/82] *Wicaȟanȟan yelo.* "There was smallpox."

Vestal states that the Tetons were camped along the Missouri at the time of the epidemic (p. 261). Battiste Good gives this event for 1779/80.[10]

19. [1782/83] *Ake wicaȟanȟan yelo.* "Another smallpox epidemic."

Battiste Good gives this for 1780/81.[11]

20. [1783/84] *Ota cuwita ṭa pelo.* "Many died from the cold."

According to Vestal, the Miniconjous were moving camp over the high prairie from one stream valley to another when a blizzard caught them. One by one the older people succumbed to the cold (p. 261).

21. [1784/85] *Sina luta in wan ahiktepi.* "They came and killed 'Wears-a-red-blanket.'"

---

[7] Mallery, *Picture Writing of the American Indians*, p. 307.
[8] *Ibid.*, p. 308. [9] *Ibid.*, p. 307.
[10] *Ibid.*, p. 308. [11] *Ibid.*

Battiste Good gives this event for 1782/83.[12]

22. [1785/86] *Topa wakte akli yelo.* "Four returned home after counting coup."

23. [1786/87] *Isna wica ẑuya ṭa kli yelo.* "Lone-man, a warrior, came home dead."

White Bull explained to Vestal that Lone-man was the leader of a war party of which three were killed. He was ridiculed for looking to his own safety and abandoning his men (p. 261).

24. [1787/88] *Heyoka wan ahiktepi.* "They came and killed a clown."

This man was a Miniconjou.[13] Vestal says that the clown was leading an attack against the enemy, but halfway he turned and fired on his own people (p. 262).

25. [1788/89] *Kanĝi ota ṭa pelo.* "Many crows died."

This year's event refers to the bird rather than the Indian tribe. The winter was intensely cold and many crows died. Battiste Good gives this event for the same year.[14]

26. [1789/90] *Řėwaktokta winyan wan hi yelo.* "A Hidatsa woman came."

According to Vestal, this Hidatsa woman left her people because she had trouble with her parents. After a while the Dakotas returned her to her own people, making presents to her parents (p. 262).

27. [1790/91] *Wowapi wan makakawin̈ ayapelo.* "They carried a book around the country."

This year's event refers to the hiring of a Dakota named Red

[12] *Ibid.,* p. 309.
[13] Cf. Mallery, *Pictographs of the North American Indians,* p. 100; *Picture Writing of the American Indians,* p. 310.
[14] Mallery, *Picture Writing of the American Indians,* p. 310.

Dog as a courier to carry a dispatch to various trading posts in the Missouri country (Vestal, p. 262).

28. [1791/92] *Miwatani okiju welo.* "They camped with the Mandans."

This may be the same event mentioned by Battiste Good.[15]

29. [1792/93] *Ake om waniti pelo.* "Again they camped with the Mandans."

30. [1793/94] *Ite ciqa ahikte pelo.* "They came and killed Little-face."

Good gives this event for 1794/95 and identifies Little-face as a Pawnee, who, though of normal stature, had a small, deformed face.[16]

31. [1794/95] *Pehi hanska ska wicaktepi.* "They killed Long-hair."

Good lists this event for 1793/94 and identifies Long-hair as an enemy. The battle took place at Rawhide Butte.[17]

Page 5

32. [1795/96] *Mniyaye yuha najin ki ya pi.* "They made Has-a-bucket stand up."

According to Battiste Good, the Arikaras killed a Dakota and then propped up the dead body in their village and hung a bison paunch water pail from the corpse's hand to mock it.[18]

33. [1796/97] *Wapaha kitonla telo* "'Wears-a-warbonnet' died."

Vestal identifies "Wears-a-warbonnet" as a famous Miniconjou (p. 262).

34. [1797/98] *Pte ciqa pte san o welo.* "Little-buffalo shot a white buffalo."

[15] *Ibid.,* p. 311.
[17] *Ibid.,* p. 311.
[16] *Ibid.,* p. 34.
[18] *Ibid.,* p. 312.

The killing of an albino bison was considered a sacred event by all Plains tribes, hence the selection of this year's event.

35. [1798/99] *Wi klu śaka ota ta pelo.* "Many pregnant women died."

This winter's event probably refers to an epidemic of puerperal fever.[19]

36. [1799/1800] *Śung paha tanka nunpa pelo.*

The Dakota text is unclear. Vestal gives "Two horses with big manes captured" (p. 263).

37. [1800/1801] *Ite can ruru toka 2 num kte yelo.* "'Charred-face' killed two."

The following explanation of this event was given Vestal by White Bull: "Charred-face" was a fourteen-year-old orphan who lived with his grandmother. He was so poor that he had no bow. When enemies came, however, he chased them with the other Dakota warriors. Two of the enemy took their stand under a cut bank and bluffed the Dakota warriors, but "Charred-face" picked up a stick, rushed in, and struck them both. When he returned to the village his grandmother was singing:

> My grandson struck the enemy,
> Yet he had no bow.

From that day his tribe of Dakotas took the name *Itazipco*, or No-bows (Vestal, p. 263).

38. [1801/1802] *Wicŕanŕan yelo.* "A smallpox epidemic."

This was the second of the disastrous smallpox epidemics which struck the tribes along the Missouri. In some tribes it is said to have carried off one in every five people.

---

[19] Cf. *ibid.*

39. [1802/1803] *Śake maza aklipi.* "They brought back shod horses."

This year the Dakota captured some horses from the Pawnees which were shod with iron shoes, the first the Dakotas had seen.

40. [1803/1804] *Sung r̃ur̃ula awicaklipi.* "They brought back curly horses."

This year the Dakotas secured horses with "curly" coats from the Pawnees.

41. [1804/1805] *Tahi on akicilowanpi.* "They sing for one another using deer tails."

This year's event refers to a performance of the *Hunka*, or *Alowanpi*, ceremony of the Dakotas, that tribe's version of the widespread calumet rite.

42. [1805/1806] *Tuweya 8 śakloṙan ahi wicaktepi.* "They came and killed eight scouts."

The eight scouts were Dakotas, and they were killed by the Crows.

43. [1806/1807] *Wanbli kuwa wa i wan ahiktepi.* "They came and killed an eagle trapper."

The Dakotas, like other tribes living along the Missouri, were in the habit of trapping eagles from pit traps in which the trapper reclined beneath a screen to which bait was fastened. This year a Dakota eagle trapper was surprised by enemies while lying in his trap and was killed.

44. [1807/1808] *Mni wica ṭe lo. Wakpa waśte iyoṙloke el.* "Flood at the mouth of the Cheyenne River."

A spring flood took the lives of a band of Dakotas camped near the mouth of the Cheyenne. The water rose so rapidly that the Indians could not save themselves.

45. [1808/1809] *Jakli ṭa pelo.* "Those who came home whist-
      ling died."

This may be the same event referred to by Battiste Good for
the year 1826/27.[20] He explains that six Dakotas, on the warpath, had nearly perished with hunger, when they found and
ate the rotting carcass of an old buffalo, on which wolves had
been feeding. They were seized soon after with pains in the
stomach, their bellies swelled, and gas poured from the
mouth and anus with a whistling noise. Thus they "died of a
whistle."

46. [1809/10] *Capa ciqala ti ile yapi.* "Little-beaver's lodge
      burned."

"Little-beaver" was the name by which the Dakotas called
the French-Canadian trader Loisel, whose establishment was
located about thirty-five miles below the present Fort Pierre,
South Dakota. This was probably the first trading establishment built in the Dakota country along the Missouri. An
estimated fifteen thousand dollars worth of furs was destroyed
in this fire, an entire year's accumulation. This event is noted
on several Dakota winter counts.

47. [1810/11] *Wi aki nica pelo.* "They fought over a woman."

Vestal explains that several men were wooing the same girl,
waiting their turn to talk with her. Those waiting became
impatient, and a fight resulted (p. 264).

48. [1811/12] *Maka qa wicakte pelo.* "They killed them in an
      earth lodge."

This year's event refers to the Dakotas' killing of some
Hidatsas who had taken refuge in an earth lodge.[21]

49. [1812/13] *Mato ciqala ahiktepi.* "They came and killed
      Little-bear."

Little-bear was a Teton, and he was killed by the Hidatsas.

[20] Mallery, *Pictographs of the North American Indians*, p. 221.
[21] Cf. Mallery, *Picture Writing of the American Indians*, pp. 275–276.

50. [1813/14] *Palani śakpe 6 wicaktepi.* "They killed six Pawnees."

Vestal identifies the six as Rees (Arikaras), and they may very well have been members of that tribe, as the same word is used for Arikara and Pawnee in the Dakota language (p. 264).

51. [1814/15] *Witapahatu wan kaŕuŕapi. Tatankinyotake len tonpi.* "They killed a Kiowa by striking him on the head. Sitting Bull was born this year."

At a peace council in the Black Hills between the Dakotas and the Kiowas, a Dakota broke up the proceedings by hitting a Kiowa on the head with his war club. This is the event which marks the winter, the second notation being a personal one by White Bull indicating the birth of his uncle, the renowned Hunkpapa chief.

52. [1815/16] *Itaẓipco kin titanka otipi.* "The Sans Arcs lived in an earth lodge."

These were apparently the first earth lodges built by the Dakotas. They were at Peoria Bottom, near present Pierre, South Dakota.[22]

53. [1816/17] *Ake oti waniyetu tipi.* "They wintered in the earth lodges again."

Strangely enough, the version of White Bull's winter count published by Stanley Vestal gives an entirely different event for the year after the Sans Arcs built earth lodges and before the "Lame-deer pulled out his own arrow" event below. The event included in Vestal's version is "The Stars Move," referring to the great meteoric shower of November 12, 1833 (p. 264). A comparison of this count and the numerous other winter counts in the anthropological literature reveals that there is, in fact, a hiatus at this point. White Bull's winter count takes up again with the year 1835/36.

[22] Mallery, *Pictographs of the North American Indians*, p. 109.

54. [1835/36] *Tarca huśte wan klu śloka.* "Lame-deer pulled out his own arrow."

According to Vestal, the Dakotas were afoot on the warpath and encountered enemies, also unmounted. The enemies ran, but the Dakotas pursued. Lame-deer was ahead of the others and shot an enemy. The enemy kept on running, but Lame-deer overtook him, jerked out his arrow, and used it again, killing the man (p. 264).

55. [1836/37] *Caṙa kiciẓapi kanṙi wicaśa om.* "Fight on the ice with the Crow Indians."

The Miniconjous surprised a party of Crows which was crossing a river on the ice, and killed one of them. Battiste Good gives the same event but states that the enemy were Pawnees.[23]

56. [1837/38] *Onpan ota wicaopelo wicaku wopina.* "They shot many elk after chasing them."

57. [1838/39] *Cuwila opi na ṭaca onyanklipi eyaś ni kli.* "Body was shot and left behind for dead but later returned to his people alive."

Body Butte, in the Black Hills, is said to be named after this man (Vestal, p. 264–265).

58. [1839/40] *Peji ici kte.* "'Grass' killed himself."

"Grass" was a Dakota transvestite[24] who chose the woman's method of committing suicide, by hanging himself.

59. [1840/41] *Hohe yamni wicaktepi.* "They killed three Assiniboins."

60. [1841/42] *Śunkle ska ota awicaklipi.* "They brought back many spotted horses."

---

[23] Mallery, *Picture Writing of the American Indians*, p. 320.

[24] Cf. James H. Howard, *Dakota Winter Counts as a Source of Plains History*, Anthropological Papers No. 61, Bureau of American Ethnology Bulletin 173 (Washington, 1960), p. 375.

Vestal states that these horses were captured from a Crow camp located west of the headwaters of Pryor Creek (p. 265). High Dog gives this event for the winter of 1838/39.[25]

61. [1842/43] *Wiyaka wanjila wacekiya na watakpe o i.* "One-feather prayed and charged the enemy."

One-feather, wishing to avenge the death of some of his relatives, conducted a medicine rite in which he collected an arrow from every man present. He then gave one arrow to every good warrior and begged them to fight. They agreed and set out but could not find the Crow (Vestal, p. 265).

62. [1843/44] *Pte pa tiyokna ka pi.* "Buffalo head kept inside."

The Sans Arc subband of the Tetons made medicine to bring the buffalo. Lone Dog gives this event for 1843/44.[26]

63. [1844/45] *Wazi i cankaskapi wanitipi.* "Pine tree fort winter camp."

This winter the Miniconjou subband of the Tetons built a stockade of pine logs to protect their camp. Lone Dog gives this event for 1844/45 as well.[27]

64. [1845/46] *Pse ŕti owasecapi wanitipi.* "They camped for the winter in an ash grove where there was a lot of food."

65. [1846/47] *Hekta tanhan a ha ri ca ktepi 14 years len tokakte ocastanka letan Tatankiyotake.* "They killed them from the rear. Sitting Bull, who was fourteen years old at the time, counted his first coup."

Returning from a battle, the Dakotas got strung out. The enemy crept up and killed three stragglers.

[25] *Ibid.* p. 374.
[26] Mallery, *Picture Writing of the American Indians*, p. 281.
[27] *Ibid.*

Page 6

66. [1847/48] *Optaye nonpa onyanklipi eyaś nina kli.* "'Two-herds' was left behind for dead but later returned home safely."

67. [1848/49] *Waśan wakpa cuwita ṭa.* "'Hole-creek' froze to death."

This man went hunting and was caught in a blizzard. His parents later found his horse and his body (Vestal, p. 265).

68. [1849/50] *Peji wanica waniyetu welo.* "A shortage of grass this year."

69. [1850/51] *Wanase ta natan hi yelo pahazizipelo i itoka r̈atan el. Chief White Bull len tonpi.* "They were charged upon while on the winter bison hunt south of Slim Butte. Chief White Bull was born this year."

Vestal notes that two Dakota hunters were killed in this encounter (p. 266).

70. [1851/52] *Ptehicala winunrcala wan ikpi knanapica apelo.* "A buffalo cow was killed and an old woman was found in its belly."

This macabre event is also found in the Lone Dog count.[28] It is famous in Dakota tradition.

71. [1851/52] *Wakpamnipi tanka canha san el omniciye.* "A big council at the White-bark place."

This year's event refers to the great treaty council at Fort Laramie.

72. [1852/53] *Waniyetu waśma.* "Heavy snowfall winter."

73. [1853/54] *Jar r̈e opta śina klekler̈a ahi waniyetu.* "'Jar' [Jordan?] brought Navaho blankets over the mountains."

---

[28] *Ibid.,* pp. 282–283.

This year's event refers to the introduction of Navaho blankets among the Dakotas.[29]

74. [1854/55]   *Matohitika ktepi okiciye na el itancank in heca.* "They killed brave-bear. He was a warrior and a chief."

According to Vestal, Brave-bear and another Dakota were killed by Assiniboins near Slim Buttes (p. 266).

75. [1855/56]   *Putihi ska wa a ksiju.* "Gray-beard detained them."

This year's event refers to General William S. Harney's holding prisoner the Dakota women and children captured in the attack on Little-thunder's camp (Vestal, p. 266).

76. [1856/57]   *Hetopa wa alowan hi yelo.* "'Four-horns' came to sing."

This man, Chief Four-horns, was Sitting Bull's uncle, and in the ceremony referred to, he adopted Noisy-walking-elk as his son (Vestal, p. 266).

77. [1857/58]   *Kanri wicasa 10 wikcemna wicaktepi Mnikowoju kin.* "The Miniconjou killed ten Crow Indians."

This battle took place at Captive Butte.

78. [1858/59]   *He wanjica wakicagelo.* "One-horn's giveaway (after the ghost-keeping)."

This year's event refers to the redistribution of goods which takes place one year after the death of a child whose spirit has been "kept" in the *Wakicagapi* ceremony.[30]

79. [1859/60]   *Kangi tanka iyo hi ktepi 2 kici ahiktepi.* "They came and killed Big-crow and two more besides."

[29] Cf. *ibid.,* p. 283.
[30] Cf. Frances Densmore, *Teton Sioux Music,* Bureau of American Ethnology Bulletin 61 (Washington, 1918), pp. 77–84.

80. [1860/61] *Ti ša ya wan kutepi Kangi wičaša oti ca.* "They killed several Crow Indians who were living in a red tipi."

81. [1861/62] *Pte ota waniyetu.* "Many buffalo [cows] winter."

82. [1862/63] *Wiyaka luta ektepi le Hohe ca waniyetu.* "They killed Red-feather, an Assiniboin."

Vestal describes this event, which occurred at the mouth of Red Water, in some detail (p. 267). Lone Dog states that Red-feather was a Miniconjou.[31]

83. [1863/64] *Šakloran ahi wicaktepi.* "They came and killed eight men."

Battiste Good states that some of the eight were Cheyennes, the remainder Dakotas.[32]

84. [1864/65] *Kangi wicaša 4 tom ewicaktepi Mnikonwoju kin.* "The Miniconjou killed four Crow Indians."

85. [1865/66] *Kangi wakuwa ozuye ta ta.* "Chasing-crow died on the warpath."

86. [1866/67] *Akicita opawinge wicakte pelo.* "They killed a hundred soldiers."

This year's event refers to the Fetterman fight of December 21, 1866.

87. [1867/68] *Caŕsu waniyetu.* "Ridged ice winter."

A quick freeze, following a thaw, left the snowbanks in fantastic, sculptured shapes.

88. [1868/69] *Itazipco ake zaptan 15 ahi wicakte pelo.* "They came and killed fifteen Sans Arcs."

Vestal describes this event in some detail (p. 268). Long-fish, a Lower Brulé, was also killed in this engagement with the Crows.[33]

---

[31] Mallery, *Picture Writing of the American Indians*, p. 285.
[32] *Ibid.*   [33] *Ibid.*, p. 326.

89. [1869/70]   *Kaṅǵi wicaśa kin 30 wikcemna yamni ewicaktepi.*
      "They slew thirty Crow Indians."

90. [1870/71]   *Canku wankatuya ahiktepi Mnikowoju.* "'High
      hump,' a Miniconjou, was killed."

This may be the same man referred to as "High Back Bone"
by Battiste Good.[34] He was killed in a battle with the Shoshonis
in the Big Horn Mountains (Vestal, p. 268).

91. [1871/72]   *Itoye hanskela ahiktepi 4 topapi Mnikowojupi.*
      "Long-forelock was killed. Four Miniconjous
      were killed in all."

92. [1872/73]   *Ska akanyanka wan ektepi Kaṅǵi wicaśa heca*
      "They killed a man riding a white horse. He
      was a Crow Indian."

This battle took place at the headwaters of the Little Big
Horn.

93. [1873/74]   *Ciqala tawicu kici ṭapi. Slota om kiciẓapi* "'Little'
      and his wife died. They fought the 'Slota'
      [Plains-Ojibwa mixed-bloods]."

From Vestal we learn that "Little" and his wife were a very
old Dakota couple. He was a shaman, and as he expired a
small bird left his mouth (p. 269). The battle with the "Slota,"
or "Grease people," has no connection with the death of
"Little" and his wife, but is merely another important event
which occurred at this time. The battle took place on the
Rosebud River, where the métis had come to hunt bison.

94. [1874/75]   *Tiyo kata iyeyapi Hunkpapa ca hecunpi Kaṅǵi
      wicaśa ca heca.* "The Hunkpapas shot into a tipi
      and killed a Crow Indian."

Vestal reverses the situation in his interpretation, stating
that a Crow Indian shot into the tipi and killed a Dakota
(p. 269).

---

34 *Ibid.*

95. [1875/76] *Ŗe sapa i waklakapi. He wanjica ṭa.* "They counciled concerning the Black Hills. One-horn died."

This year the Dakotas signed a treaty ceding the Black Hills. According to Vestal, One-horn was a Miniconjou shirt-wearer who signed the treaty and later died of shame because of it (p. 269).

96. [1876/77] *Ŗe sapa iwoklakapi śankakan wicokinpi owak-pamni el el.* "They counciled concerning the Black Hills. They took their horses away at the various agencies."

97. [1877/78] *Ta śanke witko ktepi capapi.* "They killed Crazy Horse by stabbing him." Crazy Horse, the famous Dakota leader, was stabbed in the back when he attempted to resist being imprisoned at Fort Robinson.

Page 7

98. [1878/79] *Cetan inyanke ktepi.* "They killed Running-hawk." Vestal notes that this man was a Miniconjou scout (p. 270).

99. [1879/80] *Mato kute inyankapi ahiktepi.* "They came and killed 'Shoots-bear-running.'"

According to Vestal Shoots-bear-running was killed while stealing horses from the Crows between the mouth of the Tongue River and the Powder River (p. 270).

100. [1880/81] *Taceje wakpa el akli wanitipi śunkakan wicakipi. Pte ota yelo.* "They wintered on the Tongue River and their horses were taken away. There were many buffalo this year."

101. [1881/82] *Inyan wosla el akli wanitipi. Pte ota yelo.* "They wintered at Standing Rock. There were many buffalo this year."

102. [1882/83] *Cante witko ṭa. Pte ota yelo.* "Crazy-heart died. There were many buffalo this year."

Vestal states that Crazy-heart died of despair (p. 270).

103. [1883/84] *Tatanka wanbli kaśkapi. Pte ota yelo.* "'Eagle-bull' was imprisoned. There were many buffalo this year."

Vestal notes that Eagle-bull was imprisoned because he had taken three white poachers into custody (p. 271).

104. [1884/85] *Cekpa nunm ṭapi.* "A pair of twins died."

The version of White Bull's count given by Vestal gives another event, "Crow King died," for this year (p. 270).

105. [1885/86] *Kinyan hiyaye ṭa.* "Flying-by died."

Flying-by was one of the six hereditary chiefs of the Miniconjous (Vestal, p. 270).

106. [1886/87] *Waniyetu waśma.* "Heavy snowfall winter."

107. [1887/88] *Hetopa ṭa itancan heca Hunkpapa.* "Four-horns died. He was a Hunkpapa chief."

Again, the version of White Bull's count given by Vestal gives a different event, "Dish-face died" (p. 270).

108. [1888/89] *Wi sapa ṭe lo Hunkpapa.* "Black-moon died. He was a Hunkpapa."

This man was Sitting Bull's uncle. Vestal gives a different event, "Measles epidemic" (p. 270).

109. [1889/90] *Wicarpi yamni wawokiye hi waniyetu.* "Three-stars came and counciled."

General George Crook came to the agency to secure a cession of land.

110. [1890/91] *Tatankinyotake ktepi. Onpakleśka ota ṭapi.* "They killed Sitting Bull. Many-spotted-elk died."

Sitting Bull was killed by a detachment of Indian police from Fort Yates. Many-spotted-elk, a Miniconjou, was killed by soldiers at Pine Ridge.

111. [1891/92] *Owakpamni el wamanunpi ateyapi ki hecon rca.* "Someone stole funds at the agency. The agent did it."

112. [1892/93] *Wata yuhala ktepi wawayuspa heconpi.* "'Has-a-boat' was killed by policemen."

"Has-a-boat" was the Indian name of a squaw man named Fielder. He was killed while resisting arrest by the Indian police.

113. [1893/94] *Sunkakan wokajuju icupi.* "They were paid for the horses taken from them."

This year the Dakotas were paid, in part, for the horses which had been taken from them in 1876.

114. [1894/95] *Peji wanica waniyetu.* "No grass year."

115. [1895/96] *Supe owotanla ta.* "'Straight-gut' died."

116. [1896/97] *Wicarcala ota ta pelo.* "Many old men died."

117. [1897/98] *Cannumpa wakan kin icu ateyapi hecun.* "The agent confiscated the sacred pipe."

This year's event refers to the sacred calf pipe, the principal medicine object of the Dakotas, at that time kept by a man named Elk Head. The agent at the Cheyenne River Agency, Peter Couchman, ordered the pipe confiscated by five Indian policemen. White Bull, at that time a member of the Indian police himself, was prevailed upon by the Elk Head family to intercede, as he was admired by the elders of his tribe for his bravery and fair-mindedness. White Bull agreed, and called upon the agent, who consented to have the bundle returned to its keeper. The five policemen who took the bundle from Elk

Head were ordered to return it, which they did. According to tradition, all five died within the next few days.[35]

118. [1898/99] *Wanbli kleška ṭe lo canqi la.* "'Spotted-eagle' died ——— [?]"

The latter part of the Dakota text is unclear, though the first part refers to the death of Spotted-eagle, the same event given for this year by Vestal (p. 271).

119. [1899/1900] *Kangi wicaša ahi waniyetu.* "Crow Indians came this year."

This year a group of Crows, the old enemies of the Teton Dakotas, came for a friendly visit, a clear indication of how the times were changing.

120. [1900/1901] *Mara ska ta wicaŕanŕan.* "White-swan died of smallpox."

White-swan was one of the six hereditary chiefs of the Miniconjou subband of the Teton Dakotas.

121. [1901/1902] *Pte san hunka kaškapi.* "They imprisoned White Bull."

This year's event refers to the time Chief White Bull was placed in the guardhouse by the Indian agent for insisting upon better terms in the leasing of Indian land (Vestal, p. 271).

122. [1902/1903] *Wanbli ota wicaktepi.* "They killed many eagles."

The eagles were killed on the Cheyenne River Reservation.

123. [1903/1904] *Rapid City oškate wayuštan July 4.* "A big celebration took place at Rapid City on July 4."

---

[35] J. L. Smith, "A Short History of the Sacred Calf Pipe of the Teton Dakota," *Museum News* (the W. H. Over Dakota Museum), Vol. XXVIII, Nos. 7–8 (July–August 1967), pp. 9–10.

124. [1904/1905] *Śunkakan cuwita ṭapi ota rci* "Many horses froze to death. Very many indeed."

125. [1905/1906] *Kinyukanpi Pte san hunka ṭa. Marpiya parta he wanjica ṭa.* "Makes-room White Bull died. Cloud bundle [?] One-horn died."

White Bull notes here the passing of his father, Makes-room. I have been unable to learn anything concerning the other man.

126. [1906/1907] *Pte san hunka sapa wicaśa awicayuspa waniyetu.* "White Bull brought back the 'Black men' [Utes]."

This year's event refers to the time when the government sent White Bull to persuade the Utes to keep the peace at the time of a threatened uprising (Vestal, p. 272). The Utes are termed "Black men" in Dakota because of their swarthy complexions.

127. [1907/1908] *Pte san hunka ake sapa wicaśa kin awicakli waniyetu.* "White Bull brought the Utes home again."

The events noted for this year and the previous one are described in detail in Vestal's *Warpath*, Chapter 24. Several hundred White River Utes, under their leaders Appah, Soccioff, and Red Cap, left the Uintah and Ouray Agency in Utah and came to the Cheyenne River Reservation. In June, 1907, White Bull led these Utes to his home, where the government had leased lands for them for a period of five years. While White Bull was looking after these Utes he married a Ute girl. The marriage lasted about a year, until the Utes returned to their reservation at White Rocks, Utah (Vestal, p. 249).

128. [1908/1909] *Canřařake ṭe lo. Tokala ře ki wiyope yape.* "'Hump' died. They sold Fox Butte."

129. [1909/10] *Hi hangi ṭelo.* "Yellow-owl died."

130. [1910/11] *Canpa wakpa el řе sapa um omniciye tanka.* "There was a big conference at Cherry Creek concerning the Black Hills."

The object of this council was to recover damages for the loss of the Black Hills.

Page 8

131. [1911/12] *Can pta ye ṭa.* "A man named 'Wood-pile' died."

This man, according to Vestal, was one of the best fighters of his generation (p. 272).

132. [1912/13] *Mato wakpa el wapayapi waniyetu.* "There was a fair at Bear Creek."

133. [1913/14] *Wowapi wan yu wan kol otke yapi wanbli paha el.* "They raised a flag at Eagle Butte."

134. [1914/15] *Heraka pa ṭe lo Cante wanica ṭelo waniyetu.* "Elk Head and No-heart died this year."

Elk Head was the keeper of the sacred calf pipe of the Dakotas.

135. [1915/16] *Cankařa ṭe lo waniyetu.* "'Short-log' died."

136. [1916/17] *Mato wakinya ṭe lo.* "'Bear-thunder' died."

137. [1917/18] *Wamu jica yuha ṭe lo.* "'Has-a-bob-tail' died."

138. [1918/19] *Wayaẓanpi wica ṭa ota ṭa pelo.* "An epidemic killed many people."

This year's event refers to the influenza epidemic which swept the United States and Canada this year.

139. [1919/20]   *Koki ṭa Wan anatan ṭa.* "'Koki' died. 'Charging' died."

140. [1920/21]   *Kanṛi okute el omniciye ṛe sapa on.* "Another council concerning the Black Hills was held at Crow-shooting-place [Crow Creek]."

141. [1921/22]   *Ṛe sapa iwoku wawicaka rni rapi oyanke oyasin el el.* "Black Hills treaty delegates were elected from each district."

At this time the Dakotas chose their attorney in a suit for damages for the Black Hills region.

142. [1922/23]   *Lakota tawe kinyapi hi wanbli paha el.* "The new Commissioner of Indian Affairs came to Eagle Butte."

143. [1923/24]   *Ṛe sapa kin caje yal yasupi Lakotapi ki ee pica.* "The Dakotas entered a claim for the Black Hills region. Proof of damages was offered."

144. [1924/25]   *Caje ciyorpe yapi oyaṇke oyasin el el.* "They had an election in all districts."

145. [1925/26]   *Pte rcaka taniṛa ota icuwelo Pte san hunka eca Ite sankiya ṭa.* "White Bull secured many entrails after a butchering. Paints-his-face-white died."

146. [1926/27]   *Maka wikli olotapi canpa wakpa el.* "They put in a claim for oil rights at Cherry Creek."

Again for this year the version of White Bull's count given by Vestal lists a different event, "White Bull visits the Custer Battlefield" (p. 273).

147. [1927/28]   *Ta šunke luzahan ṭa.* "Fast-horse died."

148. [1928/29]   *Wanbli šake ṭa.* "Eagle-claw died."

149. [1929/30] *Ře sapa el oškate tanka Rapid City, S.D. Pte san hunka el oitancan on.* "There was a big celebration at Rapid City, South Dakota. White Bull was chosen to make the speech of welcome [for President Coolidge]."

150. [1930/31] *Lakota wi ki kni pi waposi wan hi 1930 lem 1931 July 4 lehanska.* "An investigator came to look into their affairs in 1930. It is now July 4, 1931."

This year's event, the final one in this version of White Bull's winter count, refers to a senatorial investigation of the Indian Bureau. The final remark concerning the date is probably meant to indicate that the count was complete up to that date. There are thirty-three blank pages following this page, whereupon White Bull begins an account of some of his hunting experiences.

PAGE 9 BUFFALO AND BEAR HUNTING

Ehanna Ptercaka wanase a i na wana makiyutapi wanji wahecetuya wana Buhilkapi ca el owapa yelo mitawa kin lila luza helo tehanye rci tokeya Pte ki iwicahunni miye Pte kin wanji wao welo wahikpe on lila kakpa iye wa yelo ehanni waniyetu miye 21 years hehan yelo ake waniyetu 19 years hehan miye waniyetu ca wanase a i na wakuwapa ca owapa na ake Pte wan wahikpe on wao kakpa iyewa yelo lila waniyetu lena makeca etu 25 years etu welo henake ca kakpa ye wicawayelo Pte ki hecetu welo kola ito yupta yelo epin kte lo waniyetu lena makeca 20 etan ka hena ki ya mato kin ake wanjila ll wicawaowelo Řesapa el ihu ku on tipi eceylo el mato ota pelo he on hecetu welo kola le miyeca Chief White Bull Pte San Hunka

Lakota woecun wašte keyapi lena e e wawecaǵe lo nahan šunkakan 12 ake num ena na wicaša kin wicawaqu welo hitoska wan itancanyan el wanji e yelo nakun micincapi kin owicalo wan pelo hunka pelo šunkakan kin šakloran pelo 8 canpa kmiyanyan ciqala

sapa wan opewaton ca teca ko welo lena wicawaqu welo kola ake
micinca wanji tonpi ki 9 lenakeca pelo lena 9 el el otuwaran yelo
hikna tonpi ki el otuwaran yelo 3 yamni el wanji cincatonpi el el
4 topa otuwaran yelo otuwaran yelo opawinge wanji isam wikcemna tom ake num 1.42. lena śunkakanpi capelo micinca yuke ci
hetan han yelo mitawicu yukeci hetanhan waniyetu miye 23 years
letanhan kin 57 lehanl hi ki 1931 Aug 13 epelo. Pte san hunka
miye yelo len wo an wana 81 years kolapila.

Many years back there was a buffalo hunt. At that time we
charged the herd and I was in the thick of things. My horse was a
fast one and I reached the herd before the others. Soon I was
right in the midst of the herd and I shot an arrow at a buffalo
beside me. The arrow went right through his body and came out
the other side. That was many years back when I was twenty-one
years old. Another time, when I was nineteen, we went on a winter
hunt. Again, during the run, I shot an arrow right through a
buffalo cow. This happened to me again when I was twenty-five.
The arrow went right through the animal. This is true, I did it
just as I say I did. When I was twenty years old I went bear
hunting and killed 11 bears. It was in a place at the foot of the
Black Hills. There were lots of bears there. It is the truth. I am
Chief White Bull, Pte san hunka.

The Dakota said that this was good and to commemorate the
occasion I staged a giveaway. I gave away twelve good horses.
The best of these was a gray. I had my children sung over in the
Hunka ceremony, and each time I gave away many things. I
bought eight horses and a little black buggy and gave these to
those who had sung for my children. When my first child was
born I gave away nine horses at the giveaway. When he married
I gave away three horses. When their first child was born I gave
away four horses. I did this at a big feast I gave for them. All
together, during my lifetime, I have given away 142 horses. I did
this to honor my children. I have been married since I was twenty-
three years old, and my wife and I have been together fifty-seven
years now, August 13, 1931. I am chief White Bull, and am eighty-
one years old today.

White Bull's bear hunts are described by Vestal in some
detail in *Warpath* (pp. 151–153).

PAGE 10   ROLL CALL OF THE CHIEFS

Lakotapi el wicaśa itancanpi lena Mni wojupi el
Kinyukanpi Pte san hunka	1
Wahacanka-sapa	2
He-wanjica	3
Herloreca-ska	4
Maraska	5
Kinyanhiyaye	6
Tarca huste | lena yus lena tanyan	1
Wi-sapa | Wicakuwapi kta itancanpi kin	2
lena wicape kin ogle on pelo	

Oyate el taku iyukcanpi kin hena ecela okna on pelo oyate kin
Ehanni mni no woju oyatepi el wicaśa kin lena wicaśa yatapi itancanpi hecapi onpelo tka wana oyasin ṭapi na cincapi eyake ośtan
wicaqu pelo lena e e pelo cajepi kin epica

Kin yukapi le cinca Pte san hunka lena 6	1
Wahacanka sapa le cinca kangi tanka	2
He wanjica le cinca marpiye pato	3
Herloreca ska le cinca mato-ciqala	4
Maraska le cinca Maraska	5
Kinyan-hiyaye cinca nica	
Tarca huste le cinca Cante-witko	6

Wi-sapa itaye wara
Icincapi kin lena ake itancan onpi lena
Ake wana oyasin ṭapi Kinyukanpi cinca wan
Pte san hunka ni on nahan rci itancan on welo
Waniyetu lenakeca wana 81 len 1931 August 12
Owicoïan mitawa ota bluha yelo kola mara kota he on

The following men were chiefs of the Miniconjou:

1. Makes-room White Bull
2. Black Shield
3. One-horn
4. White-hollow-horn
5. White-swan

6. Comes-flying
   Lame-deer   Both of these men were renowned.
   Black-moon   They were treated as chiefs because of
                this. They wore shirts decorated with
                scalps [i.e., they were shirt-wearers][36]

The tribe thought a great deal of these men and followed their orders. The old time Miniconjou tribe had good leaders, men of high repute. Now they are all dead and their children have taken their places. Their descendants are named as follows:

1. Makes-room's son was White Bull   (these six)
2. Black Shield's son was Big-crow
3. One-horn's son was Blue-cloud-head
4. White-hollow-horn's son was Little-bear
5. White-swan's son was also called White-swan

   Comes-flying had no children

6. Lame-deer's son was Crazy-heart
   Black-moon [remainder of passage untranslatable]

The children of these men were again chiefs. Now all of these, too, are dead except myself, the son of Makes-room. This year I am eighty-one years old, August 12, 1931. I have followed this path and have done the many things recorded here because I am a Lakota, my friend.

PAGE 11 (*Plate 1*)   WHITE BULL COUNTS COUP FOR THE FIRST
                       TIME

The pictograph shows White Bull, dressed in a buckskin war shirt, long red breechcloth, and leggings, and armed with

[36] A shirt-wearer, or head councilor, was a man who was entitled to wear the true scalp shirt. These were made of mountain sheep skin decorated with scalps and quillwork bands. Some were painted blue on the upper half and yellow on the lower. Others were red and yellow, respectively. The shirt-wearers also wore a single eagle feather horizontally at the back of the head. (Clark Wissler, *Societies and Ceremonial Associations in the Oglala Division of the Teton Dakota*, Anthropological Papers of the American Museum of Natural History [New York, 1912], Vol. XI, Pt. 1.)

a lance and what appears to be a quiver of arrows, stabbing a cavalry trooper who is firing at him with a carbine. White Bull is mounted on a blue-colored horse which has been decorated with wavy red lines running up the legs, probably to represent lightning, and undoubtedly connected with White Bull's personal medicine. The horse wears a charm, probably a small bundle of herb medicines, with an eagle feather, attached to its neck. This charm was probably designed to make the horse invulnerable to bullets.

A dead or wounded cavalryman lies on the ground below the trooper who is fighting with White Bull. This figure probably represents the same trooper after he fell from his horse.

Akecita [*sic*] om kicizapi napapi na wicakuwapi na le hecamon welo. Tokeya wakte yelo. Waniyetu ake šakpe etu 16 years miye Pte san hunka Chief White Bull. Šunkakan kin le hito kin le lila rci luza heci heca yelo / le tokeya yelo Řeska wan el tu welo wiyořpe yata ekta yelo 16 years miye wicaša ota a i yelo kola.

[Below the man on the ground the text reads:] Le e e caparpe lo. Mato sika hunkpapa okihe kte yelo.

When I was sixteen years old I accompanied a war party that fought with the soldiers. They retreated and we chased them. During this battle I counted my first coup on an enemy. I, Chief White Bull, was sixteen years old at the time. I was riding a steel-gray pony at the time, one of the fastest I have ever owned. I was ahead of the others. This was the first time I counted coup. This battle took place out west at a place called White Mountain. Many went along on this war party, my friend.

[The portion of the text beneath the pictograph of the man on the ground may be translated as follows:] This is the stabbed one. A Hunkpapa named Bear's-foot counted second coup on him.

Although different in many of the details, this is apparently the same fight Vestal describes in *Warpath* (pp. 43–46). It took place in August, 1865, at Gourd (Pumpkin) Buttes. The "soldiers" were Omaha Indians serving as scouts in the cavalry. Because they wore their hair short in the white man's style, White Bull and his companions did not scalp them.

PAGE 12 (*Plate 2*)   WHITE BULL COUNTS FIRST COUP ON AN OMAHA SCOUT

The pictograph shows White Bull dressed as in the preceding pictograph and riding the same horse. Again he is stabbing a cavalryman who is firing at him with a pistol. Below the mounted cavalryman is the figure of what is obviously intended to be the same trooper after he has fallen from his mount.

Pte san hunka le e e le parpe lo tokeya wakteyelo tašunke witko sunka ku qun he okihe kte yelo waniyetu ake ma šakpe etu welo hito ki le lila luza he lo. Ate wahukeza le micarelo he on tokakipešni wasu miciyelo 2 le inupa yelo 16 year miye
[Below the fallen figure the text reads:] Le e e ca wapařpe lo

This is White Bull knocking another man off his horse, killing him, and counting first coup. The younger brother of Crazy Horse counted second coup. I was still only sixteen years of age at that time, and was riding my fast steel-gray horse. My father had made the lance I used on this occasion. When I took it from him I pledged that I would not be afraid so long as I carried it. This was the second man I killed. I was sixteen years old at that time.
[The text beneath the fallen figure may be translated:] This is the one I knocked off his horse.

In *Warpath* (pp. 42–43) White Bull recounts that the scout fired at him at point-blank range, but missed. He kept threatening White Bull with his pistol after this but at the same time tried to escape his relentless pursuer through flight. Finally he fired again, but at the same instant White Bull stabbed him in the shoulder with his lance, shoving him from his saddle. Cloud-man, the younger brother of Crazy Horse counted second coup on the fallen Omaha.

PAGE 13 (*Plate 3*) WHITE BULL COUNTS SECOND COUP ON A SCOUT

This pictograph is much the same as the preceding two. In this case, however, White Bull is apparently touching a cavalry trooper with his lance. The trooper has already been shot in the back with an arrow.

Pte san hunka le e okihe wakte yelo. Mato watakpe Itazipco ki le kte yelo miye waniye [*sic*] 16 years omake śakpe etu welo

This is White Bull counting second coup. Charging-bear, a Sans-arc, counted first coup. I was sixteen years old at that time.

From Vestal (p. 44) we learn that this event actually took place before those just described, on pages 11 and 12 of White Bull's sketchbook. Charging-bear was the first to overtake the fleeing scouts. He struck the man across the shoulders with his bow, then veered away from the threat of the trooper's gun. White Bull, plunging through the dust at his friend's back, counted second coup on the Omaha scout with his lance.

White Bull's Dakota text presents an interesting linguistic idiosyncrasy in his contraction of the word *waniyetu*, "winter" or "year," into *waniye*.

PAGE 14 (*Plate 4*) THE BATTLE AT GREASY CREEK

The pictograph shows White Bull in the act of counting coup on a dismounted Indian by touching him with his bow.

The enemy is discharging a pistol at him, and other Indians, crudely sketched at the left of the page, are firing at him.

Pte san hunka le e e le tokeya wakte okihe kte śni oterike lo waka onka ca wa waśpe lo. Waniyetu 18 years leta welo. Omake śakloran elu itokarata waśun wakpa ki heciya yelo Wicaśa ota a i yelo kola lena on ocaśtanpi hecayelo lakotapi el el kola lila makute pelo ma opi śni yelo

This is White Bull counting first coup. No one was able to claim second coup; it was too hard. I knocked the enemy down and scalped him. I was eighteen years old at that time. It was down south on the South Platte [Greasy Creek in Lakota]. Many men went on this war party and I became well known for my brave deed, friend. Many of the enemy shot at me but I was not wounded.

This encounter is described in detail in *Warpath* (pp. 91–92). It was one of White Bull's narrowest escapes. A war party led by Crazy-heart had attacked a camp of houses and tents occupied by both whites and Indians. The main group of the attacking party went after the horse herd, but White Bull and Crazy-heart charged two of the enemy who were near the creek instead. Before they could reach them, a great many people came out of the houses and tents and began firing at the pair. Crazy-heart, who was chasing the second enemy, turned back, but White Bull persisted. Though the enemy was armed with both bow and arrows and a gun he was so terrified he offered no resistance, and fired his gun into the air.

White Bull closed on the enemy, raised his bow, and struck the man a heavy blow on the head, thus counting coup and knocking him down at the same time. White Bull jumped from his horse but did not have time to kill the enemy. Instead, he scalped him alive, remounted, and hurriedly rode off. As White Bull galloped away, he noted that the man got up and staggered off, perhaps to die later.

By now the main force of the enemy was in full pursuit of the attacking Dakotas, and White Bull was at the very rear, nearest them. It seemed they would surely catch him, as his horse was slow. Worse yet, at this moment, of all times, White Bull's horse played out and stopped in its tracks, heaving and gasping. White Bull jumped off and ran on afoot. He was offered a hand by Thunder-bull, who had noticed his dangerous situation, and White Bull swung up behind his friend.

The enemy kept on coming, however, and Thunder-bull asked White Bull to get down, as one horse could not save them both. White Bull jumped to the ground and ran on afoot once more, until Bull-head, who had a better horse than Thunder-bull, took him up behind.

It was a close shave for White Bull. He was the only one of the party to count coup or take a scalp.

PAGE 15 (*Plate 5*) WHITE BULL COUNTS COUP IN THE FETTER-
MAN FIGHT

In this pictograph we see White Bull riding down a fallen soldier who has an arrow in his back. White Bull wears a dark shirt and a red war cape. He is armed with a bow and arrows and a lance. With the feathered butt-end of this lance he is counting coup on the fallen trooper.

Pte san hunka le e e tokeya wakte yelo. Waniyetu omake śakowin etu welo akicita opawinge wicaktepi etu welo. Okicize teri ke lo 17 years.
[Below the fallen trooper additional text reads:] Mazakan kin le iwacuwelo.

This is White Bull counting first coup. I was seventeen years old at the time. One hundred soldiers were killed in this battle. It was a fierce fight. I was seventeen years old.
[The additional text may be translated:] I confiscated this rifle.

The Fetterman Fight takes its name from Captain W. J. Fetterman, an officer who, though he had never fought Indians, often boasted that "with eighty men I can ride through the whole Sioux Nation." On December 21, 1866, the Dakotas lured Fetterman and exactly eighty men into ambush from old Fort Kearny. None returned. The Dakotas suffered to the extent of 185 killed and wounded.[37]

Vestal provides an excellent narrative account of White Bull's participation in the Fetterman Fight (pp. 50–69) and describes the particular incident above on page 63. In this battle White Bull charged a single cavalry trooper who was at the rear of his unit, facing the Indians, running backward and yelling at the top of his voice. The man was armed with a carbine, but White Bull shot him through the heart with an arrow. The man fell on his back and as he did so White Bull cracked him across the head with his lance, counting first coup. The rifle (Vestal says it was a carbine) was captured later in the battle.

PAGE 16 (*Plate 6*)   THE WAGON BOX FIGHT

The pictograph shows White Bull mounted on a steel-gray horse which has golden eagle tail feathers attached to the mane and tail. He is wearing a full buckskin costume, plus a red war cape and a flaring eagle-feather bonnet. In his hand he carries the decorated lance emblematic of the second in command of a war party. Representations of hoofprints in a great arc indicate that he rode close to the enemy as an act of bravado. At the left are represented three men with rifles. They are drawn between two wooden buildings with windows, doors, and chimneys. Five horizontal marks at the right are probably intended to indicate flying bullets.

Pte san hunka le e ti ska ki yapi etu waniyetu 17 years miye. Okicize tanka ca oklakla inyanka ca lila kute pelo.

[37] John G. Bourke, *On the Border with Crook* (Chicago: Rio Grande Press, 1962 [reprint of the 1891 edition]), pp. 291–292.

This is White Bull at the Battle of White House. I was seventeen years old. It was a big running fight and there was a lot of shooting.

Of all the battles in the Indian Wars, none, except the Battle of the Little Bighorn, has received more attention than the Wagon Box Fight. This engagement took place near Fort Phil Kearny on August 2, 1867. The battle involved an estimated one thousand Tetons and Cheyennes on the Indian side against thirty troopers under the command of Captain James Powell and First Lieutenant John Jennes. The Dakota attempted to repeat the decoy and ambush tactics of the Fetterman Fight, but these failed. They therefore attacked a woodcutters' camp about five miles west of the fort. The troopers, armed with the latest breech-loading rifles and seven thousand rounds of ammunition, were stationed in wooden wagon boxes formed into a corral at the camp.

The Dakotas and Cheyennes made four separate attempts to rush the wagon-box corral, but each time were driven back by furious fire from the defenders. The Indians kept up an attack on the corral for three and a half hours before a relief column from the fort, equipped with a howitzer, was sighted and the chiefs called off their men. Six Indians were killed and six wounded, while six men were killed on the white side. The health of many of the troopers, including Captain Powell, was broken by the strain of the experience. (Vestal, pp. 70–83)

It is interesting to note that White Bull includes only one pictograph of this battle, which is made so much of by white historians. His reason for terming it the "Battle of White House" is not known.

PAGE 17 (*Plate 7*) WHITE BULL COUNTS COUP ON A CROW BUNDLE OWNER

The pictograph shows White Bull mounted on a black stallion. He is wearing only a breechcloth and moccasins and is armed with a bow and arrows. Five Indians wearing the enemy hairdo (that is, the pompadour and long back hair customarily worn by the Crow, Hidatsa, Blackfoot, and other tribes often at war with the Dakotas) are firing at him. Below White Bull's horse is the prostrate figure of a dead man identified in the text as a Crow Indian. Below this man and also to his left is a dotted line, evidently a representation of footprints. These connect with a round object, identified in the text as a sacred bundle made of a white buffalo hide. To the right of the picture are several hoofprints and a crescent of similar hoofprints to indicate the path of White Bull. Short, dark streaks surrounding White Bull and his steed indicate that he rode out before the enemy under intense fire from the Crow.

[At the upper left of the page the text reads:]
   Kiyukarpi lecinca
   Tatankiyotanke tonśkaku welo
   nakun hecetu lena
   okitanni rcelo
[The principal text reads:] Pte san hunka e e le kahi rpe ya kici takici kpea pi na kanǵi wicaśa pelo tokeya wakte yelo okicize tanka yelo Pte san ha ca le qi u cokam u ca kokipapi ca hecamon welo. Waniyetu 20 years etu śunkakan ki le lila luza he lo hunkpapa yapi kin wanyankapelo tuki wakpa iyorlo ke etu welo okitan inyan woecon welo okitan inyan woecon welo kola opi śni ca wicohan ki kle lo
[By the white buffalo bundle the text reads:] le Pte san ha ca qi u welo icupi na ya bla yapelo wanblakelo
[Below the fallen enemy the text reads:] Kanǵi wicaśa pelo

[The text at the upper left of the page may be translated:]
   Son of Makes-room
   Nephew of Sitting Bull
   They will verify this great deed.
[The principal text may be translated:] This is White Bull running down an enemy. This was at a battle with the Crows and both sides stormed each other's lines. I counted first coup in this great battle. One of the Crows was carrying a sacred bundle consisting of a white buffalo hide. He came out between the lines to encourage his men and everyone was afraid to go out and kill him.

Finally I did it. I was twenty years old at the time and was riding an unusually fast horse. The Hunkpapas saw me do this. The battle took place at the mouth of Shell Creek. They praised my deed, friend. I was not wounded and came back safely to our own lines.

[The text written by the picture of the white buffalo bundle may be translated:] They took this white buffalo hide and spread it out and I saw it.

[The text written below the fallen enemy may be translated:] It was a Crow Indian.

This battle, known as the Fight-over-the-white-buffalo-hide, took place at the mouth of the Musselshell River in 1868. Early in the fight White Bull was knocked senseless when a Crow rifle bullet narrowly missed his head and cut one of his braids, just below the right ear. Recovering, he angrily galloped back into the battle, determined to get even. Noticing a man with a sacred bundle tied to his back, he furiously rode the man down and counted first coup on him by striking him with a saber. Three other Dakotas also counted coup on the man, who escaped with his life but abandoned the sacred bundle he was carrying. The Crows counterattacked in an attempt to recover this sacred relic, but failed. In addition to the sacred white buffalo hide, the bundle contained some bones. (Vestal, pp. 98–101)

Though this bundle is not one of those mentioned in Wildschut's recent study of Crow medicine bundles,[38] it was clearly a war medicine bundle and in its simplicity quite typical of the Crows.

PAGE 18 (*Plate 8*) WHITE BULL COUNTS COUP ON A FLATHEAD

This pictograph shows White Bull mounted on a steel-gray horse and armed with a rifle or carbine. He is pursuing an

[38] William Wildschut, *Crow Indian Medicine Bundles*, ed. John C. Ewers, Contributions from the Museum of the American Indian (New York, 1966), Vol. XVII.

enemy who is mounted on a brown. The enemy warrior's horse has been wounded twice, as indicated by red wound marks in its flanks. White Bull is counting coup on the enemy by touching him with a feathered banner of the type commonly associated with the Strong-heart and Crow-owners warrior societies. The enemy is firing at him with a pistol. Numerous hoofprints are shown.

[Above the pictographs the text reads as follows:] Pte san hunka le e natablecapi heca okicize tanka rca tokeya wakte lo kuwa onka upi tka wakawire na wica wakuwana le wakte yelo waniyetu 21 years hetu welo miyeca nakun nupa el iye wayelo wanmayake ci ota pelo kola lena on ocaśtanpi ki heca yelo kola lakotapi el.

[Below the pictographs the text reads:] Lila nakipapelo natable-capi lena napapelo. Okicize tanka wan el tokeya toka ktepi kin le wankatuya ke ya pelo lakotapi ki heyapelo le ecel ecamon welo waśte yelo kola

[Near the head of the enemy's horse the text reads:] Natan upi lenake pelo

This is White Bull counting first coup in a big battle with the Flatheads. They chased us but I turned back and chased them and succeeded in counting coup. Then I shot at him twice. Many saw me perform this deed and because of it I was highly honored by the Lakotas, my friend.

[The text below the pictograph is in two sections. That at the left may be translated:] They really ran. The Flatheads really ran. [At the right it reads:] There was a big fight and this was the first man killed. Because of it I was highly praised by the Lakotas. It was a glorious fight, my friend.

[The text above the head of the enemy's horse may be translated:] They were charging me from this direction.

A group of forty-three young Tetons were trying to decoy the Flatheads into ambush. White Bull, eager for war honors, lagged behind, baiting the pursuing Flatheads. All alone, he turned his horse back and charged his enemies. One of the

akecita o Wi kici papi nepapi na Wicakuwipi na ta hecaWan Wicto tokeyaWatteyelo
Winniyate Ole dobleete. Waysaremiye. Pte San humka chief White Bull.
SunkaKanKu le kito Kii le lila rei luyyn hee peeoyelo   16 year Wi'xe
le tokeyayelo ReshaWan el tee yelo Winyoke yata akkuyelo
Wicasa ota oayelo hola

                                                              le ee capaxyelo
                                                    Mato ciko humlopla o kike klayelo

↑ Plate 1   ↓ Plate 2

Pte San humka le ee apaxyelo to keya Whktteyelo ∄ taiyykl Pitte Sunbahee yunky
okike klteyelo Winniyate ole maiyahyeete. rakya pityui te wanwepatego
ate Winku Re yaki le Wi ca to relo ite on toko ki fewii Wahar Wikiyelo
2 ee inupayelo
                                    16 year miye

                                          le ee cawkfkaxyelo

Pte san hunka lee oki he unkte yelo Mato Witakpa itanjka
ki le hte yelo Miye Waniya 16 years a Make's at the ete Wela

↑ Plate 3   ↓ Plate 4

Pte San hunka lee le to keyon na ta tan pani oki he
pte hni ota niko lo Waka ou ca ca wa wa ya le lo
yuni ya lo 16 years late wela
a Make Sakko nan ete to ta le to ota niwu ngka
lehe i ya lo Tute ya lo ota oin cho hola
cena on ca's con'ka kecaya lo lalo ta pi el el hala
lee Waseete ya lo na gli hni yelo

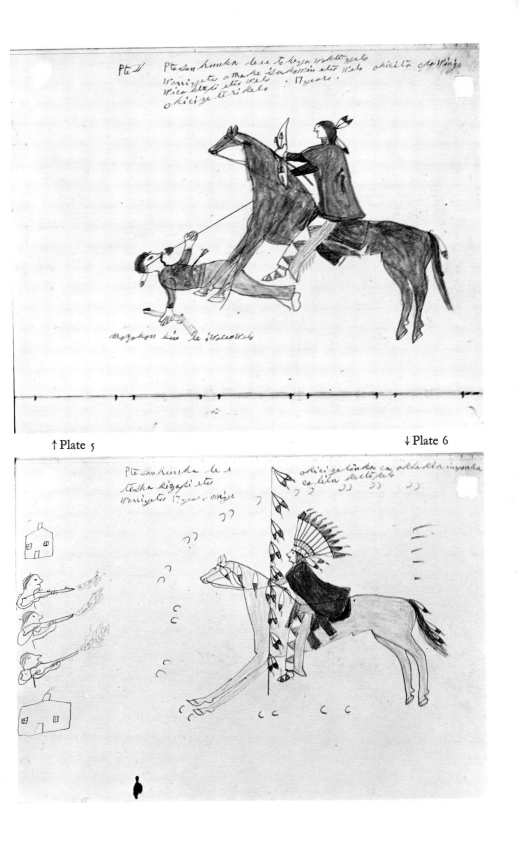

↑ Plate 5

↓ Plate 6

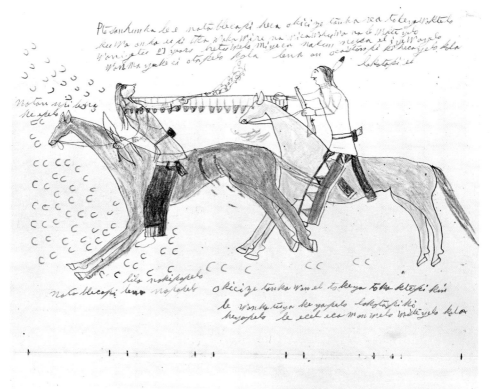

↑ Plate 7   ↓ Plate 8

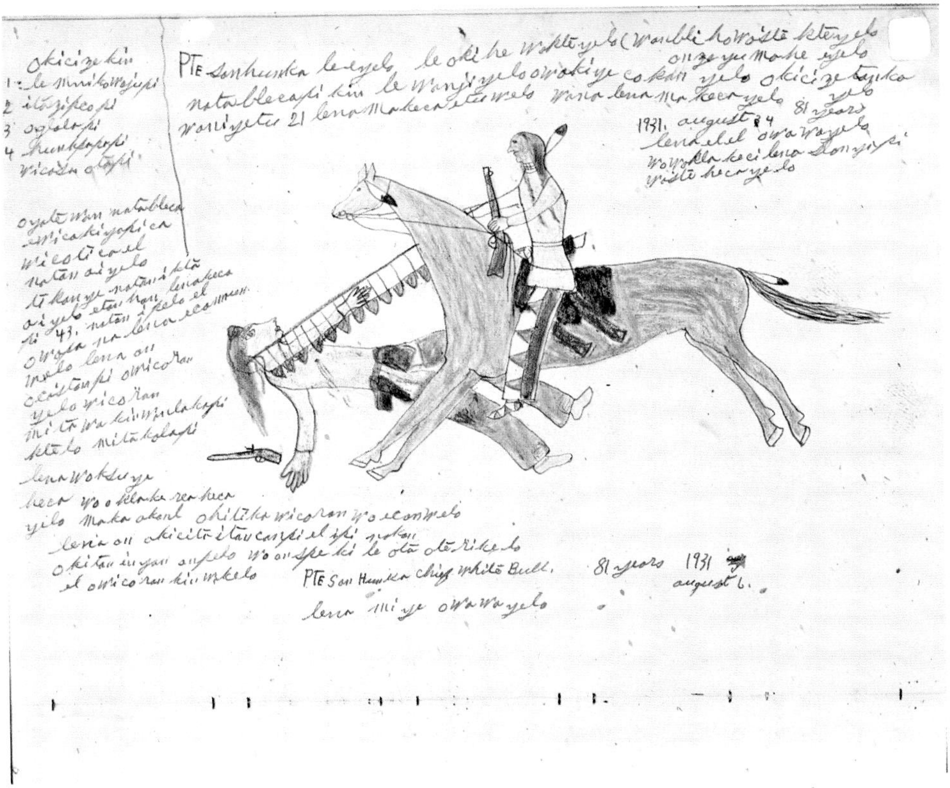

PTe Sanhunka le ecela, le oti he wakte yelo (wanbli ho waste kte yelo
notable capi kin le wanji yelo owakiye co kan yelo okicize tanka
oni za ye make yelo okicize tanka
wani yeta 21 lena Makecate wi kelo vana lena mni heca yelo

1931, august 4   81 years
lenahiel owa wa yela
woyaka kei lena kon ye yi
yi ste heca yelo

okicize kin
1 le mni kowaji cpi
2 ito zi kce pi
3 oyala pi
4 huwa pota pi
wicoran ota pi

oyate wan notablec a
wicaki yoji ca
wicasa te cael
notan oi yelo
to kan ye notan i pin
oi yelo etan kon lena peca
ti 41, notan pa lena ecom wan
owala pa lena ecom wan
yelo lena on
cayta pi owicoran
yelo wicoran
mi to pru kin mni lakepi
pte lo mita kolapi

lena wo ksuye
heca wo oklaka rea heca
yelo maka oken okitiha wicoran yo ecom yelo
lena on okicita e tan canki el zpi notan
okitan iuyan su pelo wo onspe ki le ota ote kikelo
el owicoran kin mkelo   PTe San Hunka chief white Bull.   81 years 1931
august 6.
lena imi ye owa wa yelo

↑Plate 9   ↓Plate 10

mni ko wiji wan   PTe San hunka   le wakte to keya au ni wa te ika
kiyu kan ki lecai ca   ma o zni ca waste yelo notable capi
tatan ki yo toke le tan Skakee white Bull. he iwaji eyelo
ate stancan kin heca kin on stoko ki na zni' wa au kta wacin ecaiyelo
le ote kigla eso nan welo makute eyes' ma o zni yelo yi'a sto yelo owakiye co kan yelo
ohokan tehan rei naji yaya yelo   okicize tanka kelo   wani yeta 21 years etu mi ye
le ote ki yo woecon yelo Bluha yelo kola   vana lena makeca wakte yelo

81 years. 1931 august 6.
le woni yi ki tehani
yi kelo heca
kinyan yu haye kola

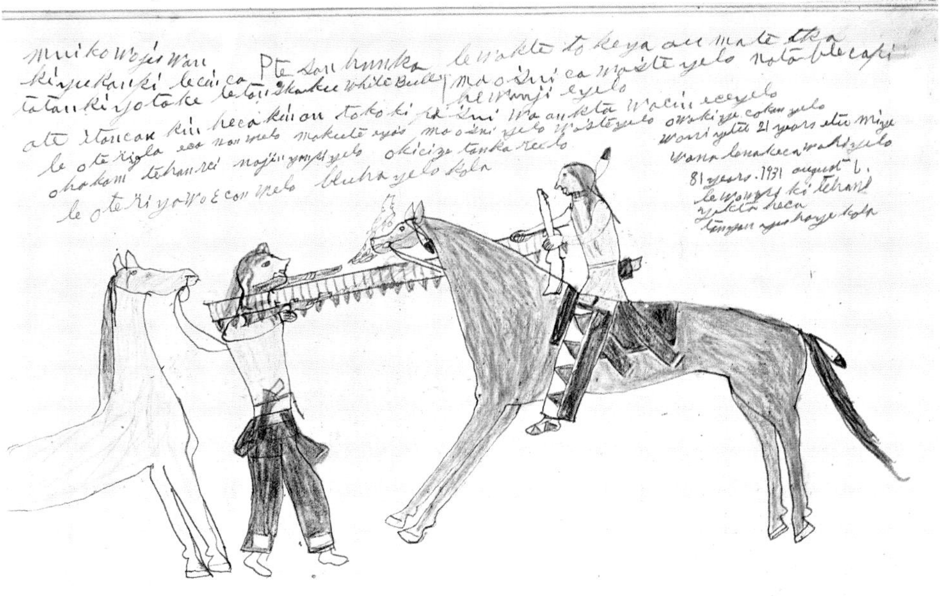

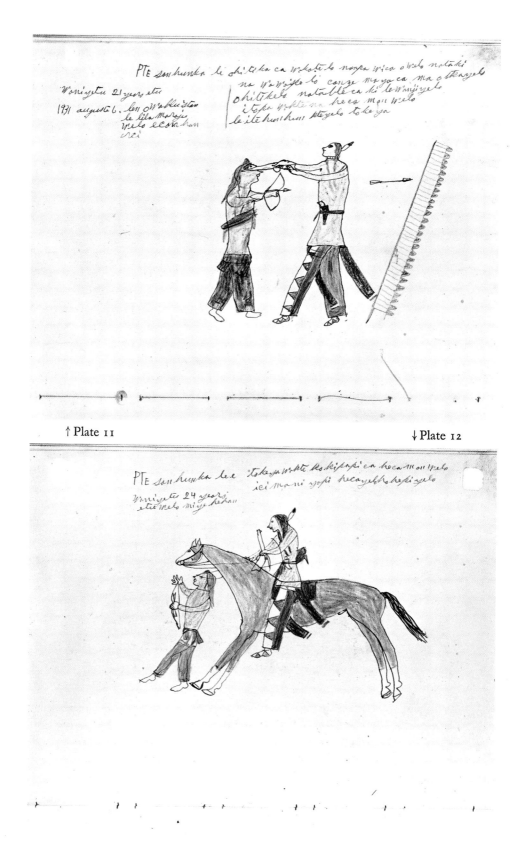

PTE san hunka le ohi'ti ka ca wikote lo naxpa wica oikelo natáki
na Wawijilo lo canze me yo ca ma otkeazelo
ohititkelo natable ca ki le Winijiyelo
i'topa wikte na heca mon melo
le ite hunhun stoyelo to ke yo

Woniyetu 21 years etu
1931 auguste 6. lecn Wablu istan
le lila Maraji
melo ecomhan
nei

↑ Plate 11   ↓ Plate 12

PTE san hunka lee   tokex wikte Ro kipapi'ca heca mon melo
ici mani yapi hecayelo hepi yelo
Woniyetu 24 years,
etu melo miye kehan

Wanígtela sunkawiyela
Waniyetu 26 years.

1931 august 7

Waniyetu 81 years

le otéri yelo
kola

Pehinhanska
akicita yelo

Chief White Bull.
Pte san hunka

Flatheads in the rear waited for White Bull. White Bull struck the Flathead three times with his lance and finally shot the man's horse down. He thought he had his enemy, whose leg was pinned beneath the fallen steed, but the man extricated himself and escaped by running in among the tents where White Bull could not reach him. Curiously, according to Vestal's account both White Bull and the Flatheads were armed with revolvers rather than rifles or carbines. (Vestal, pp. 119–120)

PAGE 19 (*Plate 9*) WHITE BULL'S BRAVEST DEED

The pictograph shows White Bull, dressed and armed as in the preceding pictograph, counting coup on a dismounted enemy. The enemy is in the act of discharging a rifle at him.

> [At the upper left of the page the text reads:]
>   Mni ko woju wan Kiyukanpi le cinca
>   Tatankiyotake le tonśkaku
> [The text beginning at the center of the page reads:] Pte san hunka White Bull le wakte tokeya au mate tka ma o śni ca waśte yelo natablecapi he wanji eyelo. Ate itancan kin heca kin heca kin on tokokipeśni wa ankta wacin eceyelo le oteŕci yelo ecamon welo makute eyaś ma o śni yelo waśte yelo owakiye cokan yelo ohanhan tehan ŕci najin yanpi yelo okicize tanka ŕci lo le oteŕi ya woecon welo bluha yelo kola
>   Waniyetu 21 years etu miye wana lenakeca wahi yelo 81 years 1931 August 1. Le wowapi ki tehanl yakta heca tanyan yuhaye kola

> [The text at the upper left of the page may be translated:]
>   Son of Makes-room, a Miniconjou
>   Nephew of Sitting Bull
> [The text beginning at the center of the page may be translated:]
> White Bull counted first coup. They shot at me but didn't hit me.

That was good. It was one of these Flatheads that I counted coup upon.

My father was a chief and because of this I showed no fear. It was because of him that I wanted to be in the thick of the fight. It was a hard thing to do but I accomplished it. They were all shooting at me but they didn't hit me. I was right in the middle of things.

Afterwards they [the enemy] pursued me a long way, clear back to my own lines [?]. It was a great fight. I did this difficult deed and count it among my coups, friend.

I was 21 years old at the time, and have come a long way since. Now I am arriving at eighty-one years, August 1, 1931. This book looks back at those times. Take good care of it my friend.

This event occurred shortly after that pictured on White Bull's page 19. White Bull charged one of the pursuing Flatheads who was armed with a rifle, using only his feathered lance. White Bull struck the enemy on the head, but the Flathead ducked the blow and fired at the same instant. The blow spoiled his aim. He missed White Bull but the bullet broke the lance shaft and cut away one of the eagle feathers with which it was decorated. The deed is reckoned as the bravest of all White Bull's coups. (Vestal, pp. 120–121)

PAGE 20 (*Plate 10*)   THE ATTACK ON THE FLATHEAD CAMP

This pictograph shows White Bull dressed and armed as in the two preceding pictographs. He is counting coup with a feathered lance upon a fallen enemy who has a bullet wound in his chest.

[The text beginning at the upper left-hand corner of the page reads:]
Okicize kin
1. le Mnikowojupi
2. Itazipcopi
3. Oglalapi

4. Hunkpapapi
Wicaśa otapi
Oyate wan natableca ewicakiyapi ca wicoti ca el natan a i yelo
tikanye natan i kta a i yelo etanhan lenakeca 43. Natan i pelo el
owapa na lena ecamon welo lena on ocaśtan pi owicoïan yelo
wicaïan mitawa kin wanlakapi kte lo mitakolapi lena woksuye
heca wo o kla ke rca heca yelo maka akanl ohitika wicoran
woecon welo lena on akicita itancanpi el ipi nakan akitan inyan
anpelo woonspe ki le ota oteïike lo el owicoran kin wakelo

> Pte san hunka Chief White Bull
> lena miye owawayelo
> 81 years 1931 August 6.

[The text beginning at the center of the page reads:] Pte san
hunka le eyelo le okihe wakte yelo Wanbli howaśte kte yelo
Onze yumahe eyelo natablecapi kin le wanji yelo owakiye cokan
yelo okicize tanka yelo waniyetu 21 lena makeca etu welo wana
lena makeca yelo 81 years 1931 August 4 lena el el owawayelo
wowokla keci lena slonyanpi waśte heca yelo

[The text beginning at the upper left-hand corner of the page
reads:]
Those who fought:
1. The Miniconjous
2. The Sans Arcs
3. The Oglalas
4. The Hunkpapas
There were many men.
There was a tribe we call the Flatheads. They had a camp and
we attacked it. We charged close to the tipis and they came out.
Forty-three were in the party that charged the camp and I was
among them when I did my brave deed. This was a noted event.
Many saw me performing this act [i.e., counting coup], my
friends. They remember the deed and will vouch for my truthful-
ness. Throughout the land people praised my deeds. Many war
chiefs went on this party, men who have become famous, and
they know the many difficult deeds that I performed.

> Pte san hunka Chief White Bull
> I wrote this myself
> Eighty-one years of age, August 6, 1931.

[The text beginning at the center of the
White Bull counting the second coup (Good-
first coup. He was also called His-rectum-
was fighting with one of the Flatheads righ
struggle. It was a fierce fight. I was twenty-
time. Now I am eighty-one, August 4, 1931. 1
All of this I am describing the people know at
good.

The man upon whom White Bull struck second coup was
the same Flathead that had almost killed him earlier in the
fight. Someone else had killed the enemy, and Good-voiced-
eagle and White Bull were now counting coup on the corpse.
(Vestal, p. 121)

PAGE 21 (*Plate 11*)   HAND-TO-HAND COMBAT WITH A FLAT-
HEAD

The pictograph shows White Bull, dressed and armed as in
the three preceding pictographs, but without his horse. He is
engaged in hand-to-hand combat with an enemy warrior. This
enemy has fired one arrow at him and missed, and is preparing
to fire another. White Bull is shooting his enemy in the head.
White Bull's feathered lance stands behind him unused.

Pte san hunka le ohitika ca wakate lo nonpa wica o welo nata ki
na wawoṡpe lo canze mayaca ma o tka yelo ohitikelo natableca ki
le wanji yelo itopa wakte na hecamon welo le ite hun hun kte lo
tokeya
[The text at upper left reads:] Waniyetu 21 years etu 1931
August 6 len owabluṡtan le lila maraju welo econhan rci

This is White Bull doing a brave deed. I killed one of the
enemy, shot him twice in the head, and scalped him. He made me
mad because he almost hit me [with an arrow]. He was a Flathead,

a brave man. I counted fourth coup and did this deed. Scarred-face counted first coup.

[The text at the upper left may be translated:] I was twenty-one years old. On August 6, 1931, I finished writing this. It is raining hard right now.

This was a close call for White Bull, as his carbine jammed just as the Flathead was loosing his arrow. (Vestal, p. 122)

PAGE 22 (*Plate 12*) WHITE BULL SPARES TWO ASSINIBOINS

Here we see White Bull, dressed as before, but armed with a bow and arrows and a carbine. He rides a brown horse with a white blaze on its face and white stockings. He is counting coup on a dismounted enemy with the end of his bow.

Pte san hunka le e. Tokeya wakte kokipapi ca hecamon welo. Ici mani yapi hecayelo Hohepi yelo. Waniyetu 24 years etu welo miye hehan.

This is White Bull. I counted first coup and they were afraid of me when I was doing it. Some Assiniboins were traveling through the country. That's who it was. I was twenty-four years old at the time.

White Bull and his companions discovered the Assiniboins, a man and wife, traveling alone across the open prairie in broad daylight. The man was armed only with a bow and arrows. He resisted the Dakotas at first by threatening them with his bow and arrows, but when White Bull raised his carbine to shoot him, he lost his nerve and ran. The Dakotas counted coup on both the man and his wife, and would have killed them, but the woman cried out, "Take pity." Since the Assiniboin tongue is a dialect of the Dakota language, White Bull understood her plea. Thinking of his mother, he spared

the lives of the Assiniboin couple, and the entire group pic-
nicked together on the grass and made friends. White Bull
warned the foolish Assiniboin couple to stay in the timber
until dark and then go on their way. (Vestal, pp. 163–165)

PAGE 23 (*Plate 13*)   THE BATTLE OF THE ROSEBUD

The pictograph shows White Bull riding a roan horse which
has been decorated with "lightning" designs painted on the
legs, neck, and rump and which has golden eagle feathers tied
in the mane and tail. White Bull wears an eagle-feather warbonnet with a long single tail, a buckskin war shirt, long red
breechcloth and leggings, and his *wotawe*, or personal medicine
packet. He is in the act of firing his carbine at a mounted
enemy, who is also firing at him. The enemy's horse is wounded
in the shoulder.

[The text beginning at the upper left-hand corner reads:] Onjiji
tka wakpa el okicize etu welo okicize tanka yelo tona el onpi kin
wanmayanka pelo akicitapi na toka ocaje ota kapelo kaṅgi wicaśa
kapelo
[Beneath the preceding there is a horizontal line, and under it the
text reads:] Śahiyela oglala mnikowoju Itazipco Hunkpapaya
oyate lenakeca om okicize yelo oterikelo okicize tanka rce lo el
micajeki waśte yelo el wicořan 5 zaptan ecamon welo
[The text beginning at the top center of the page reads:] Pte
san hunka le e susunica ohitika canke cokam yerci wa on canke
le ahi ta ma kpe u ca owanji la na wanji na kin he on ko makipa
na kawir iyaya kta tka icanl ena okata ye wayelo ta śanke kin eca
wicaśa ki naji na wice kna ki kle lo owakiye cokam yelo waniyetu
lena makeca hehan 26 years wana len wahiyelo 1931 August 6.
len maraju welo le o wabluśtan yelo
[Below the pictograph of White Bull the text reads:] Le mnikowoju welo kinyukanpi W.B. cinca miyeyelo nakun tatankinyotake tonśkaku miyeyelo Wiyaka waśte win ina wayelo tatanka
wanjila sunka wayelo

[To the left and below the pictograph of White Bull the text reads:] Owotanla wowakla eceyelo cokam ece woecun ece bluha ki he on hepelo.

[The text beginning at the upper left-hand corner may be translated:] The battle was at Rosebud Creek [in present-day Montana]. It was a big fight. All those who were there saw me. Warriors and enemies of all sorts were there. The Crow Indians were there.

[The text below the horizontal line may be translated:] Cheyennes, Oglalas, Miniconjous, Sans Arcs, Hunkpapas, all of these tribes were present, fighting together. It was a hard fight, a really big battle. I lived up to my good name and counted five coups.

[The text beginning at the top center of the page translates:] This is White Bull, the other a brave Shoshoni. I was right in the center of the line and he came charging me, but I stood my ground. When he saw that I was doing this, he became afraid and turned back, but just then I shot and hit his horse. The man stood by his horse and then retreated to his own lines, where his friends gathered around him.

I was twenty-six years old at the time. Now I have come this far, August 6, 1931. It is raining outside as I finish writing this.

[The text below White Bull's pictograph may be translated:] I am a Miniconjou, son of Makes-room White Bull and the nephew of Sitting Bull. Good-feather-woman is my mother. One Bull is my brother.

[The text at the lower left of the page may be translated:] I am telling the truth. I was in the thick of the fight when I did this deed that I claim.

The events described here occurred at the Battle of the Rosebud, June 17, 1876. White Bull and other Dakotas, together with some Cheyennes, were attacking a party of government Indian scouts. The scouts, backed up by regular troops under the command of General George Crook, then counterattacked, and the brave Shoshoni was in the lead. This man fired twice at White Bull but missed. White Bull shot the enemy's horse and dropped it. He then ran the Shoshoni down and lamed him in the right leg before joining his comrades in retreat. Because of this deed White Bull was sometimes called "The-man-who-lamed-the-Shoshoni." White Bull considered the Shoshoni warriors the best he had ever fought. (Cf. Vestal, pp. 187–189)

PAGE 24 (*Plate 14*) WHITE BULL IS WOUNDED BY THE SOLDIERS

The pictograph shows White Bull riding a pinto which is decorated by having its tail clubbed in a knot and tied with a piece of red strouding. White Bull wears two feathers erect at the back of his head, a choker necklace, a buckskin shirt, and trade-cloth leggings and breechcloth. His *wotawe*, or personal war medicine, is worn bandolier fashion so as to hang under his left arm. He has been wounded twice. At the left of the page are representations of four soldiers firing at him. Hoofprints indicate that White Bull rode in a great circuit, cutting near the enemy lines as an act of bravado.

[The text at the upper left-hand corner reads:] Tatankinyotake ti el akli ma onpapelo he pejuta ma qu pi topa can rci na waste makara pelo mate eyas wani na lehan ni wa on welo kola

[The text at top center reads:] Pte san hunka le eca opelo. Akicita opelo ta he ceyas ake ni yelo na lehan ni on welo hehan waniyetu lena makeca yelo 26 years.

Wana len wahiyelo 1931 August 6. Omaka len 81 lena makeca yelo wana akicita ki ota pelo na Lakota ki ota pelo kola.

[The text at the upper left-hand corner may be translated:] They brought me back to Sitting Bull's camp. Here they gave me medicine for four days, and made me well again. I was almost dead but, as you can see, I am still alive today, my friend.

[The text at top center may be translated:] This is White Bull. The soldiers shot at me. They wounded me severely and I was nearly dead but I survived and I am still alive. I was twenty-six years old at the time. Now, August 6, 1931, I am eighty-one years old. There were many soldiers and many Dakotas involved in the fight, my friend.

This battle took place on October 15, 1876. It started when some young Dakotas rode up to a train of military wagons to beg for food, but were fired upon by the apprehensive wagon guards. White Bull joined the battle after it was in progress. He rode to within seventy-five yards of the wagons but was hit before he could count coup. The bullet hit him in the left upper arm, passing clear through and breaking the bone. The shock of the wound knocked him out, but he stuck to his horse and two friends came and led him back to camp. He carried the scar throughout his life. (Cf. Vestal, pp. 220–221)

PAGE 25 (*Plate 15*) WHITE BULL KILLS LONG HAIR (I)

This is the first of four pictographs showing White Bull's struggle with General George A. Custer, in which Custer was finally killed. White Bull is dressed much as in the preceding pictograph and is armed with a carbine. He rides a bay (red) horse and is pursuing a mounted soldier also riding a bay. The soldier is in the act of discharging a carbine which White Bull is wresting from his grasp. Beneath the two mounted figures White Bull has drawn the prostrate figure of another soldier. From the text it becomes evident that this figure also represents Custer, but at a later stage in the struggle.

[The text beginning at the upper left-hand corner of the page reads:] Śahiyelapi Oglalapi Mnikowojupi Itazipcopi Hunkpapa-yapi Owohe nupapi etanhan Sihasapapi etanhan pelo lenakecapi el. Pehin hanska el natan i na ota [?] iyeya mazakan lila wicaktepi na Lakotapi ki wana etanhan katiye wica yapi canke canyepi hik-lapi na om kicizapelo ka miś eya om ecamon welo ho hecetu welo. Kola akicitapi ki lena etan tonakeca el ṭapi heci omakiyaka wo kola.

Lakotapi ki tona el ṭa paki ociciyaki kte lo akicita om okicize na el lakota ki tonakeca el ṭapi ki oyasila owa bluha yelo kola hena yacin ki o na ran maya wo tan iyohila cajepi ki owabluha yelo kola.

[The text beginning at the top center of the page, the principal text, reads:] Pte san hunka e e le blurpe lo Pehi hanska natan hi el Pehi hanska rpa ye ci he iwihinape eci yatan han hel tokeya napapi hel wicawakuwa na el hecamon welo otan tanke el tu ca waśte yelo hehan waniyetu lena makeca yelo 26 years śunkakan ki le luza he lo okicize tanka yelo.

[The text beginning at the upper left-hand corner of the page may be translated:] The Cheyennes, Oglalas, Miniconjous, Sans Arcs, Hunkpapas, some of the Two Kettles and some of the Blackfoot [division of the Teton Dakotas] were there. All of these groups were represented. Long Hair [General Custer] charged the camp and there was a lot of confusion and gunfire. Many Dakotas were killed as a result of this first charge and this made them [the Dakotas] mad. We counterattacked. We fought with them and I was in the first assault wave. My friend, maybe you can tell me how many of them we killed. Maybe you can tell me how many Dakotas were killed. We had a great fight with the soldiers and as many Dakotas were killed [as we killed soldiers]. I have it all written down my friend, and if you want it let me know. I can name every one of our people there, my friend.

[The text beginning at the top center of the page may be translated:] This is White Bull. Long Hair came charging in but I pulled him off his horse. He was lying at the east end. At first they ran, but I chased them. That's when I did it, while the excitement was going on. It was wonderful. I was twenty-six years old at the time. My horse was a fast one. It was a great fight.

In view of the great public interest in the Custer fight it is interesting to compare the pictograph presented here with that given by Vestal opposite page 196, the top pictograph. Clearly, both portray the same event, though in his 1934 biography of White Bull, Vestal carefully concealed the identification of Custer in order to protect White Bull from possible harm.

PAGE 26 (*Plate 16*)   WHITE BULL KILLS LONG HAIR (II)

In the second pictograph of the series depicting the fight with Custer, White Bull is shown charging a dismounted trooper who is firing at him with a carbine. White Bull is dressed and armed as in the preceding pictograph, but in addition he carries what appears to be a stone-headed war club in his right hand. His horse is ornamented with a scalp dangling from the bridle which does not appear in the preceding pictograph. Beneath White Bull's horse a fallen trooper is shown, also hoofprints and a dotted line which may be intended to represent footprints.

[The text at the upper left-hand corner of the pages reads:] Kiyukanpi W.B. le cinca, nakan Tatankiyotake tonśkaku welo. Tatanka wanjila sunka wayelo. Waniyetu 26 years. Wana len wahi waniyetu 81 years 1931 August 7. Anpetu le owawa yelo kola.

[Slightly below this, between the two combatants is written:] Le oteri yelo kola.

[Below the figure of the standing trooper is written:] Pehi hanska akicita yelo

[The text beginning at the top center of the page reads:] Pte san hunka le e. Paha najin canka kokipapi tka kahirpe ya i bla ble lo a u ma te eyaś ma o śni yelo waśte yelo oteri keci le heca yelo woecon ki le kola

Taku iblu kcan ki lena wanlakapelo kola lakotapi waśicanpi ocajepe ota wanmayanka pelo na slonmayan pelo kola miye kin le Chief White Bull Pte san hunka

[The text at the upper left-hand corner of the page may be translated:] I am the son of Makes-room White Bull, and the nephew of Sitting Bull. One Bull is my brother. I was twenty-six years old. Now I have reached the age of eighty-one. August 7, 1931. I wrote this today my friend.

[The text between the two combatants may be translated:] It was difficult, friend.

[The text below the figure of the standing trooper may be translated:] This is Long Hair, the soldier.

[The text beginning at the top center of the page may be translated:] This is White Bull. He stood pointing his carbine at me and I was afraid but I charged him and ran him down. He fired at me but missed. It was lucky for me. This was a hard fight, the hardest I ever fought, but finally I overpowered him.

I have had this in my memory for a long time. Now I have shown it to you, friend. Many of the Dakotas and the white men saw me do this and know me, my friend. Chief White Bull.

PAGE 27 (*Plate 17*)   WHITE BULL KILLS LONG HAIR (III)

In this pictograph White Bull, mounted, is counting coup on the fallen Custer with his quirt. Custer is seated on the ground, and has been wounded in the groin. This pictograph apparently corresponds with the one accompanying Vestal's article "The Man Who Killed Custer" in the *American Heritage* magazine (February, 1957). In the Vestal pictograph, however, both White Bull and Custer are represented as being dismounted, and Custer is standing, not sitting on the ground.

[The text at the upper left-hand corner reads:] Kinyukanpi le cinca. Tatankiyotake tonskaku e e. Tatanka wanjila sunka wayelo nakan ate lekši misunkala lecetu welo

[The text at the top center of the page reads:] Chief White Bull Pte san hunka le e tokeya wakte yelo pehi hanska akicita yelo. Waniyetu lena makeca etu 26 years tohanni waka winge šni wa on welo lena wanmayankapi iceyelo wowicaka iceyelo owotonla yelo lenake kola

[The text at the upper left-hand corner may be translated:] I am the son of Makes-room, the nephew of Sitting Bull. One Bull is my brother, and father, uncle, and brother have verified this deed.

[The text at the top center of the page reads:] Chief White Bull counting first coup on Long Hair, the soldier. I was twenty-six years old at the time. I never turned back when I began. This deed was seen by others who will vouch for me and verify that I am telling the truth, my friend.

PAGE 28 (*Plate 18*)   WHITE BULL KILLS LONG HAIR (IV)

In this pictograph White Bull and Custer are seen grappling with one another. Behind Custer, who is on the left, is a fallen trooper with a wound in his chest, apparently representing Custer at a later stage in the fight. His carbine lies at his feet.

[The text at the upper left reads:] Kinyukanpi le cinca yelo. Tatankiyotake tonṡkaku. Tatanka wanjila sunkawayelo. Hehan wani 26 lena makeca yelo

[The text at the top center reads:] Pte san hunka le e yelo le iya warpa ye na wokate lo tokeya wakteyelo nape on nupa omapelo oyazan ma yelo nakun mayukmicelo Ica mazakan kin on waka te lo le kokipapi ca hecamon welo Pehin hanska akicita yelo

[The text at the upper left may be translated:] I am the son of Makes-room, the nephew of Sitting Bull. One Bull is my brother. I was twenty-six years old at the time.

[The text at the top center may be translated:] This is White Bull. I grabbed him and killed him. I counted first coup. He hit me with his fists and hurt me and then he grabbed my braids. I grabbed his carbine and killed him with it. I was scared but I finally succeeded. The soldier was Long Hair.

By way of commentary on the pictographs and accompanying text on pages 25 through 28 in White Bull's manuscript, we can state that in every major respect but one this account matches quite accurately those given by Stanley Vestal in his *Warpath* (pp. 198–201) and his later "The Man Who Killed Custer." In the former, to protect White Bull, Vestal refers to

Custer as merely a "tall, well-built soldier," while in the latter he identifies him, and thus identifies White Bull as Custer's slayer. The only important discrepancy between those two accounts and this one occurs in the identification of the weapon White Bull used to beat, or beat and shoot, Custer to death. Both of the Vestal accounts say that it was a pistol, yet White Bull's own account clearly identifies it as a rifle or carbine—*mazakan* in Dakota.

Because of the great interest in the incident and the details of Custer's demise, the more detailed version from Vestal's article is offered for comparison with the above account:

I charged in. A tall, well-built soldier with yellow hair and mustache saw me coming and tried to bluff me, aiming his rifle at me without shooting. I dodged it. We grabbed each other and wrestled there in the dust and smoke. It was like fighting in a fog. This soldier was very strong and brave. He tried to wrench my rifle from me. I lashed him across the face with my quirt, striking the coup. He let go, then grabbed my gun with both hands until I struck him again.

But the tall soldier fought hard. He was desperate. He hit me with his fists on the jaw and shoulders, then grabbed my long braids with both hands, pulled my face close and tried to bite my nose off. I yelled for help: "Hey, hey, come over and help me!" I thought that soldier would kill me.

Bear Lice and Crow Boy heard me call and came running. These friends tried to hit the soldier. But we were whirling around, back and forth, so that most of their blows hit me. They knocked me dizzy. I yelled as loud as I could to scare my enemy, but he would not let go. Finally I broke free.

He drew his pistol. I wrenched it out of his hand and struck him with it three or four times on the head, knocked him over, shot him in the head, and fired at his heart. I took his pistol and cartridge belt. Hawk-Stays-Up struck second on his body.

"*Ho hechetu!* That was a fight, a hard fight. But it was a glorious battle, I enjoyed it. I was picking up head-feathers right and left that day."

After killing Custer, White Bull started to climb the hill where about ten troopers were still holding out. Suddenly he stumbled and fell. His leg was numb and his ankle swollen. White Bull guessed that he had been hit by a spent bullet. He therefore crawled into a nearby ditch and hid until the few remaining soldiers were killed.

He stayed in the ditch until his friend With Horns happened by and found him. With Horns took White Bull on his own horse and led it back to the Indian camp. White Bull's father, Makes-room, called in White Bull's famous uncle Sitting Bull to treat White Bull's swollen ankle. Sitting Bull, in addition to being a famous warrior and chief, was renowned as a medicine man. To effect the treatment, he used the famous wound medicine of the Plains Indian, known as *Pó-ipìye* in Dakota (*Allionia nyctaginea* Michx., or wild four-o'clock). After he had rested a while and eaten, White Bull mounted another horse and forded the river to get his leggings and saddle, which had been left there earlier in the battle. After recovering these he rode over the battleground to see the dead. Most of the troopers' bodies were naked, having been stripped by the Indians, but White Bull did not see any that were mutilated. While surveying the battleground White Bull happened to meet a relative named Bad Soup. It was this man who definitely identified the "tall soldier" whom White Bull had killed as Custer:

> On the hill top I met my relative Bad Soup. He had been around Fort Abraham Lincoln and knew Long Hair by sight. When we came to the tall soldier lying on his back naked, Bad Soup pointed him out and said, "Long Hair thought he was the greatest man in the world. Now he is there."
>
> "Well," I said, "if that is Long Hair, I am the man who killed him." Nobody scalped Long Hair, because his hair was cut short.[39]

[39] Vestal, "The Man Who Killed Custer," p. 9.

PAGE 29 (*Plate 19*)   COUNTING COUP ON ONE OF CUSTER'S MEN

In this pictograph White Bull, on foot, is in the act of shooting at a dismounted cavalryman, who is firing back at him. The trooper also holds a second carbine in his left hand.

> Pte san hunka Chief White Bull Tokeya wakte yelo. Pehin hanska ta akicita le wanji eyelo natanipi na lila mazakan uta pelo lakotapi, etanwana katiye wica yapelo miš lila canze mahikle lo šunkakan kin owicayuštanpi na maka mani napapelo hunr nape šni najipi ca hena ena rpa yupelo lila mazakan uta pelo akicitapi kin hecetu welo kola hehan waniyetu lena makeca yelo 26 years.

> Chief White Bull counting first coup. It was one of Long Hair's soldiers. We charged them and the Dakotas were raked with a heavy fire. Many of us were killed by this volley. This made me very mad. They left their horses and fled on foot. Some did not retreat but stood their ground. We overran their position, although the soldiers kept up a heavy fire. I was twenty-six years old at that time, my friend.

This is very likely an event that occurred shortly before White Bull's duel to the death with Custer (cf. Vestal, p. 197). One of the dismounted troopers, finding the Indians all around him, stood turning from side to side, threatening them with his carbine. Though he did not dare fire, since it would leave him defenseless, he managed to keep his enemies at a distance. White Bull, however, was undaunted. He rode straight for the trooper. At close quarters the man fired, but White Bull dodged and the ball missed him. A moment later he flung the shoulders of his horse against the trooper and rode him down.

By his choice of words White Bull clearly distinguishes the trooper of this event from General Custer: *Pehin hanska ta*

17

Chief White Bull;
Pte San hunka lee

Kin yu kan pin be cinca
tatanki yo ke tou thoku ee
tatanka Wazila sunka Wo yelo nahan
ate lakci mi sun kala heetuwelo

tokeya Wakte yelo pehi han sho okicita yelo
Waniyetu lena Wakeca etee 26 years
to han ni Wako Winiza Zoni Wa on Welo
lena Wni Mni yan kpi iceyelo Wo Wicake
iceyelo Wa tancha yelo tuneke Kola

↑ Plate 17

↓ Plate 18

18

Kin yue kanpi be cinca yelo
tatanki yo ta ke tou thoku
tatanka Wazila sun Wo yelo
hehan yuni 26 lena Marke
ca yelo

Pte San hunka le eyelo le iyu Wakaya na Wakaste le
tokeya Wakte yelo nupe on nupa a Mayelo oyan yan Mayelo
nahan Mayu keWi ca lo leanza kan kin on Wakte lo
le ko kipapi ca heeannonWelo Pehan han sha okicito yelo

19.

Pte san hunka e chief White Bull

tokeya Makte yelo Pehi han ska tu okici ta
b Wanji eyelo ninta wicki na lila Magakan
uta pelo olotaki etan winna koti ge wica
yspelo Mis lila conze mahi kte lo
Tunkakan kin owicayuttanpi
na maka mani nakapelo
kyuk nyke ini' najki ca
heca ina glagupelo
lila magakan uotapelo
okicitapi kin hecate wela
kola hahan wiriyelo
lena maka ca yelo

26 years

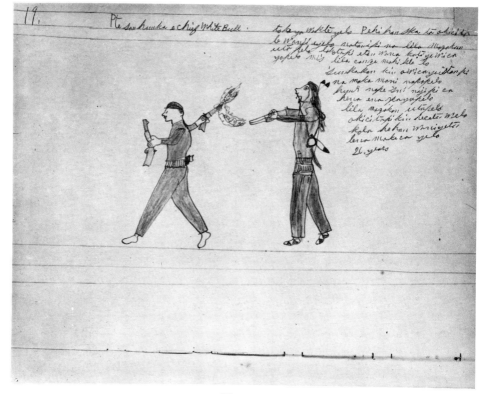

Plate 19

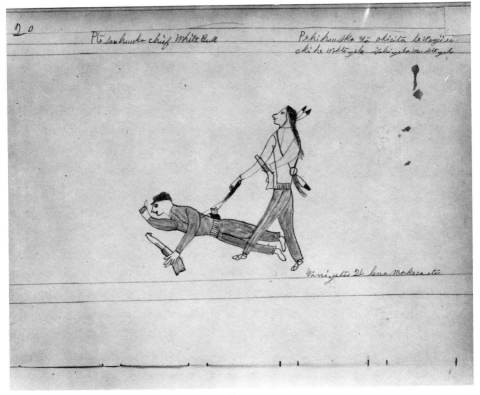

20

Pté san hunka chief White Bull

Pehi hanska ya akicita le Wasicu
akihe wakte yelo itohiyela wakte yelo

Wani yetu 26 lena Makica etu

Plate 20

2.1

Pte San hunka e   to ke ya Wakte yelo   pehin han ska to a kicita le
                                          Wanjin ayelo

lila wapiye lo el le ki ya yelo ca keca maui tte lo

2.2   Pte San hunka lee   toi sunka ki ena yoya lena ki ya ofi ki he ou
                                          Pehihan ska okicige el yayelo ote rikikle lo Ma la
Wasi yeto 26 ota   Wico ran ota ote rike lo Kolakite
                                          okicige yicoran ki ote rike yelo kolakite

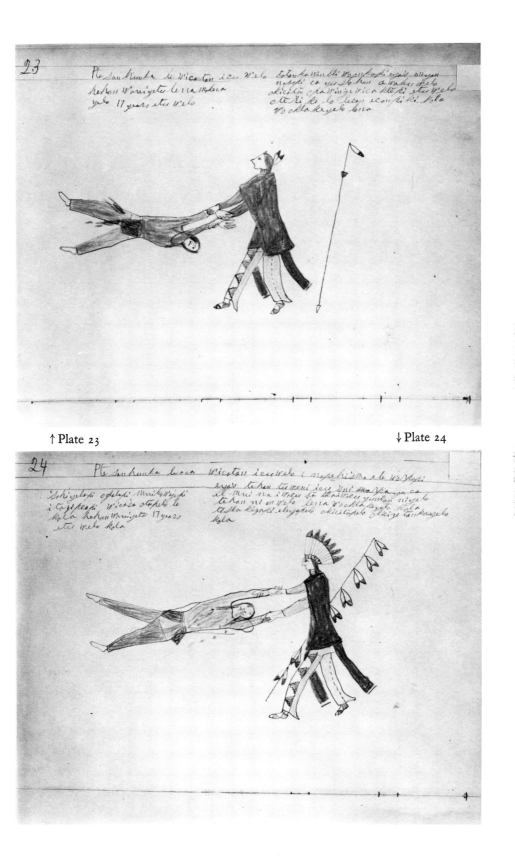

25

Pte san hunka leca Wicatanica welo (tatanka wijica nata el gleca ta ypayelo el Mni na yuslo han aWakee Welo natableca om hicignsi etes Welo kaha yujin Wau takle ye na Pte gwe han po atayela Welo hecetu Welo Kola te lo he han Wani yetes lena Makeca 21 ynoy hecetu Welo Kola le itaji pelo Welo mitaka hecan yelo

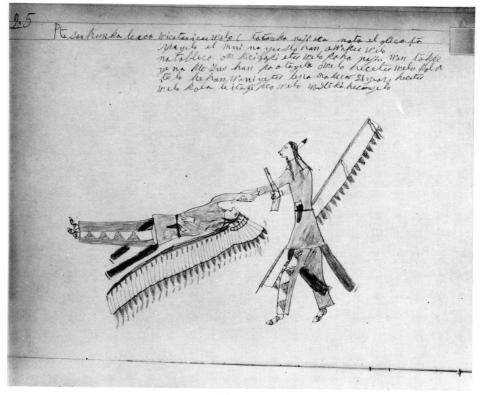

Plate 25

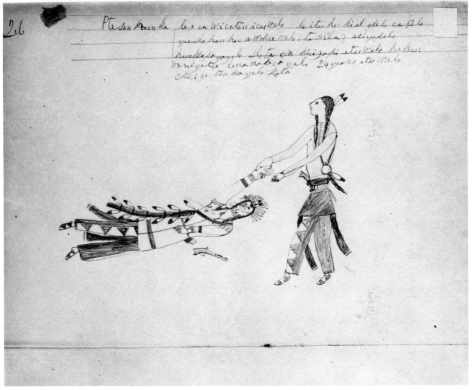

Pte san punka les en wicatan icu velo hoitu hu kiil dela ca telo
yunlo han ku a woku velo to mila, eciyakelo
hunkpa yapel Slota en kiiizapi ete velo hehun
waniyetne lenama teca yelo 24 years ete velo
okkige tanka yelo hota

Plate 26

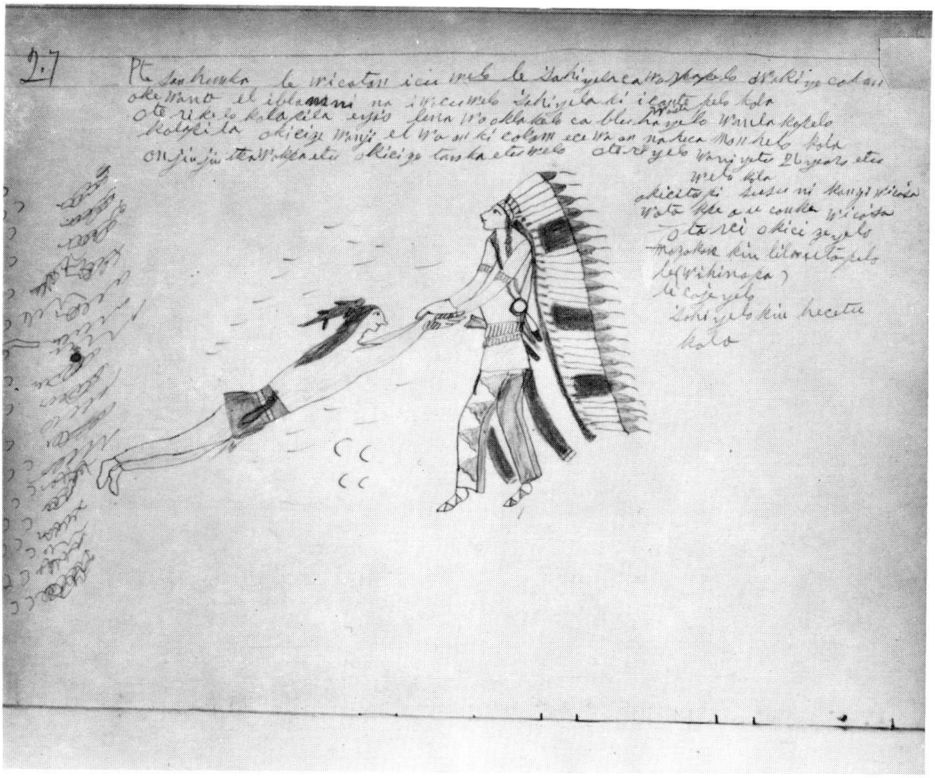

↑ Plate 27

↓ Plate 28

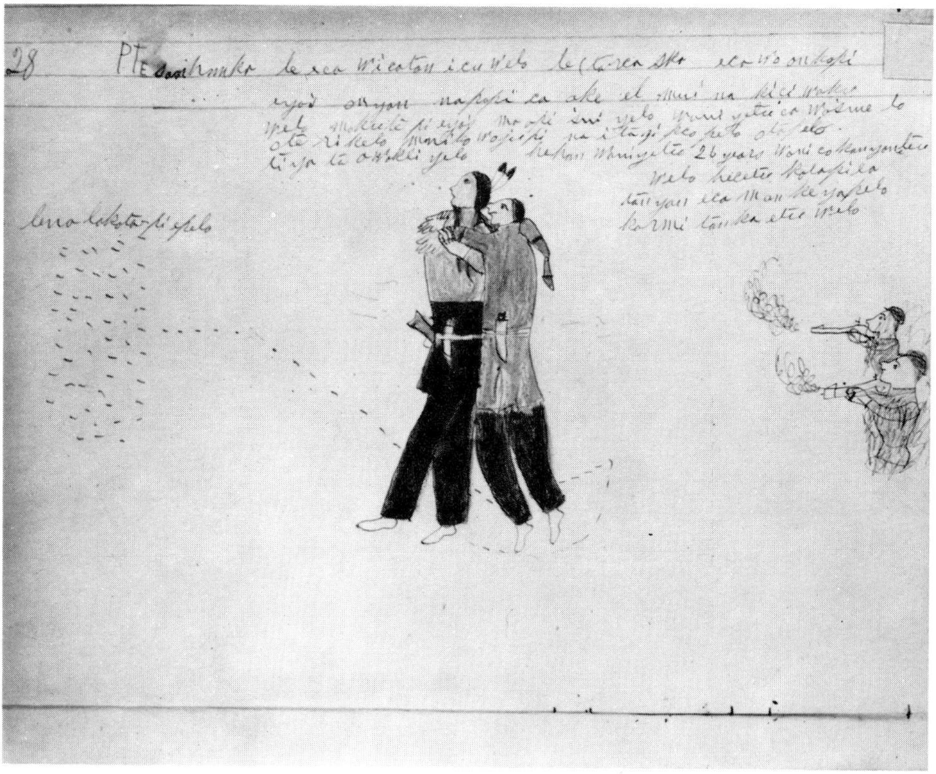

akicita, that is, "one of Long Hair's soldiers," as compared to *Pehin hanska akicita*, "Long Hair, the soldier" of the preceding pages.

PAGE 30 (*Plate 20*) A SECOND COUP IN THE CUSTER FIGHT

In this pictograph White Bull shows himself counting coup on a fallen trooper with his quirt.

Pte san hunka Chief White Bull Pehin hanska ta akicita le wanji e e okihe wakte yelo Šahiyela wan kte yelo.
[Beneath the pictograph of White Bull the text reads:] Waniyetu 26 lena makeca etu.

Chief White Bull counting second coup on one of Long Hair's soldiers. A Cheyenne killed him [and counted first coup].
[The text beneath the pictograph of White Bull may be translated:] I was twenty-six years old at the time.

This event apparently took place immediately after White Bull's struggle to the death with Custer and before he was hit in the ankle by the spent ball. It is described in Vestal's 1934 version of the affair (p. 200), but is completely omitted from the 1957 account (p. 9). According to the 1934 account, after killing Custer, White Bull was between the remaining troopers on the hill (near where the monument now stands) and the river. The troopers seemed to despair of holding their position. Ten of them jumped up and came down the ravine toward White Bull, shooting all the while. Two soldiers were in the lead, one already wounded and bleeding from the mouth. White Bull and the Cheyenne waited for them. When they came near, White Bull shot one, the Cheyenne the other. They both ran up to count coup. White Bull struck first on one soldier, but the Cheyenne beat him to the other and he got only the second coup. The eight remaining soldiers kept on coming and forced White Bull out of the ravine onto the ridge. It was then, according to Vestal's 1934 version, that White Bull stumbled and fell due to the spent ball's hitting him in the ankle.

Aside from the puzzling discrepancy between Vestal's two versions of what happened to White Bull after Custer's death, one wonders why White Bull, in the present version, mentions only the second coup, counted on the trooper killed by the Cheyenne, and omits entirely the first coup which he struck on the trooper he killed on the same occasion.

PAGE 31 (*Plate 21*)   WHITE BULL COUNTS COUP AND SECURES
A PISTOL

In this pictograph White Bull shows himself removing a pistol from the holster of a fallen trooper. A large dark spot covering the trooper's head may indicate that he has been scalped. To the left of this scene are numerous hoofprints indicating a mass retreat by the cavalry.

Pte san hunka e. Tokeya wakte yelo Pehin hanska ta akicita le wanji eyelo.
[Below the pictograph the text reads:] Lila napape lo el hirpa yelo ca hecamon welo.

This is White Bull. I counted first coup. It was one of Long Hair's soldiers.
[The text below the pictograph may be translated:] They were really running. One of them fell there and I did it.

This event took place at the Battle of the Little Big Horn. The trooper was a member of Calhoun's troop. White Bull led a charge which seemed to break the morale of the survivors of the company, and they all ran to join Keogh, every man for himself, afoot or mounted.

One of the Dakotas shot a mounted trooper and White Bull saw the man waver in his saddle. He raced forward to strike the first coup, but before he could reach the spot the dying man fell from his saddle. White Bull reined in his mount, jumped down, and struck the body with his quirt, yelling "*Unhe!* I have overcome one!" He took the dead man's revolver and cartridge belt. Did-not-go-home counted second coup on the dead trooper. (Vestal, p. 196)

PAGE 32 (*Plate 22*) WHITE BULL'S HORSE IS SHOT FROM UNDER HIM

In this pictograph White Bull shows himself mounted on a bay horse with white stockings. Three soldiers are firing at him from the left of the page, and his horse has been wounded in the withers, twice in the shoulder, and in the head. It is bleeding profusely from the mouth. Hoofprints indicate that White Bull rode close to the soldiers' lines before returning to his own.

[The text at the upper left reads:] Pte san hunka le e. Waniyetu 26 etu.

[The text at the right, which is separated from the above by a vertical line, reads:] Ta śunke kin ena rpa lena keya opi ki he on Pehi hanska okicize el rpayelo oteri hikle lo kola wicoran ota oterike lo kolapi la okicize wicoran ki oterike yelo kola pi la

[The text at the upper left may be translated:] This is White Bull. I was twenty-six years old.

[The text to the right of the vertical line may be translated:] His horse was wounded in several places and fell. It was in the fight with Long Hair that my horse was shot from under me. It was a hard fight, my friend. Many brave deeds were performed on that occasion, my friend, warlike deeds of the most difficult sort, friend.

This event occurred just after Custer's troops had turned their animals loose. White Bull had just caught a sorrel from this group of horses when his own mount was hit, and apparently the sorrel as well. In spite of the fact that his horse was shot through the foreshoulder and chest, the ribs, and the head just behind the ears, White Bull himself was untouched.

PAGE 33 (*Plate 23*)   WHITE BULL RESCUES BULL EAGLE

This pictograph shows White Bull rescuing a fallen comrade on the battlefield. White Bull wears two golden eagle feathers erect at the back of his head, a choker necklace, a dark-colored cloth shirt, and over it a red war cape. On the lower part of his body he wears a long red breechcloth and yellow deerskin leggings with a beaded strip up the side. Beaded moccasins complete this elegant costume. Behind him is his lance, ornamented with a single eagle feather at the butt and an unidentified object about a foot farther up the shaft.

[The text at the upper left reads:] Pte san hunka le wica ton icu welo hehan waniyetu lena makeca yelo 17 years etu welo
[The text at the upper right reads:] Tatanka wanbli waonkapi eyaś onyan napapi ca yuslohan awaku welo akicita opawinge wicaktepi etu welo oteři ke lo lecon econpi ki kola wo okla ke yelo lena

[The text at the upper left may be translated:] White Bull recovering the body. I was seventeen years old at the time.
[The text at the upper right may be translated:] Bull Eagle was shot down but they ran away and left him. I dragged him back to our lines. This was during the battle when we killed one hundred soldiers. It was a hard thing to do friend. I swear it.

This incident occurred during the Fetterman Fight, December 21, 1866. Bull Eagle was trying to count coup on a fleeing infantryman, but was shot in the thigh and unable to move. The fire from the soldiers was so intense that his comrades ran to cover and no one went to his rescue.

The young White Bull, a Drum Keeper of the Fox warrior society, felt a special obligation, and therefore jumped off his horse and ran out to the stricken man under fire. He seized Bull Eagle by the wrists and dragged him over the edge of the ridge to safety. There the wounded man's uncle took charge of him, while White Bull rejoined the combatants. (Vestal, p. 62)

PAGE 34 (*Plate 24*)   WHITE BULL RESCUES HAIRY-HAND

In this pictograph White Bull is again shown recovering the body of a fallen comrade. He wears a flaring eagle-feather warbonnet rather than the two eagle feathers shown in the previous pictograph but is otherwise dressed in the same way. He carries, or has near him, a lance decorated along its length with paired eagle feathers.

> Pte san hunka le eca. Wicaton icuwelo Nape hiśma e le. worpapi eyaś tehan tuweni icu śni rpa ya ca el mni na i wacu ṭa tka iwacu yunkan ni yelo tehan ni on welo lena wo okla ke yelo kola Ti ska kizapi el eyapelo akicita pelo akicize tanka yelo kola
>
> [The text at the upper left reads:] Śahiyelapi oglalapi mnikowoj-upi Itazipcopi wicaśa ota pelo le kola hehan waniyetu 17 years etu welo kola.

> This is White Bull. I brought back a body. Hairy-hand had been shot down [off his horse] and he lay there a long time but no one picked him up. Finally I went out and carried him back. He was badly shot up but he recovered and lived for a long time afterwards. I did this deed at the White House fight. It was a big battle with the soldiers.
>
> [The text at the upper left may be translated:] Cheyennes, Oglalas, Miniconjous, Sans Arcs—there were many men my friend. I was seventeen years old at the time my friend.

This pictograph and the accompanying text refer to a rescue performed by White Bull at the celebrated Wagon Box Fight, which occurred near Fort Phil Kearny, August 2, 1867. Hairy-hand, a Miniconjou, had been at the front of the charge on the corral but was shot from his horse a hundred yards south of it.

When White Bull saw his friend lying on the prairie under fire, he left his horse by the creek and ran forward afoot to save the wounded man. He found that Hairy-hand had been shot in the right breast and was bleeding from the nose and mouth. The bullet had not gone through. White Bull grabbed him by the wrists and pulled him back out of danger where Hairy-hand's relatives took charge of him. (Vestal, p. 75)

PAGE 35 (*Plate 25*) WHITE BULL RECOVERS STANDING
BUFFALO'S CORPSE

In this pictograph White Bull is represented recovering the body of a fallen comrade who wears a magnificent trailed war-bonnet. White Bull wears only a single eagle feather at the back of his head. He is attired in a brown shirt, long red breechcloth, beaded leggings, and moccasins. He carries a rifle or carbine and wears a pistol at his belt. He bears the feathered lance of the *Cante-t'inza*, or Strong-heart, warrior society.

Pte san hunka le eca wicaton icu welo (Tatanka naji eca) Nata el opi ca ta rpa yelo el mni ya yuslohan awaku welo Natableca om kicizapi etu welo paha najin wan takpe yena kte śni han pa ota yelo awe lo hecetu welo kola te lo hehan waniyetu lena makeca 21 years hecetu welo kola le Itazipco welo waśte ki hea yelo

This is White Bull. I recovered a body (it was that of Standing Buffalo). He was shot in the head and killed. He lay where he fell and I went and dragged him back. This happened in the fight with the Flatheads. One of the enemy was aiming at me but I charged out and he didn't hit me, though he fired near my head. That's how it was. I was twenty-one years old at the time, my friend. This man was a Sans Arc. It was a good deed.

PAGE 36 (*Plate 26*)   WHITE BULL RECOVERS HIS-KNIFE'S CORPSE

In this pictograph White Bull is shown recovering the body of another fallen comrade. The fallen man wears a Hudson's Bay blanket capote and the shoulder sash of one of the warrior societies. White Bull is simply dressed in buckskin shirt, breechcloth, and leggings, and has a blanket belted around his waist. He wears two eagle feathers erect at the back of his head and his *wotawe*, or war charm.

Pte san hunka le e ca wicaton icu welo le itu hu ki el opelo ca te lo yuslohan han a waku welo (Ta mila) eciyapelo Hunkpapa yayelo Slota om kicizapi etu welo hehan waniyetu lena makeca yelo 24 years etu welo okicize tanka yelo kola.

This is White Bull bringing back a body. They shot him in the forehead and killed him. I kept dragging him and finally got him back to our lines. He was called His-knife and was a Hunkpapa. This occurred in the battle with the "Slota." I was twenty-four years old at the time. It was a big fight, my friend.

The battle with the "Slota" mentioned here took place at the mouth of Rosebud Creek, near the present Rosebud, Montana, in April 1873. The Dakotas refer to the battle as "Fighting in Trenches." The "Slota" were mixed-blood Plains-Ojibwa and Plains-Cree bison hunters, otherwise known as métis. The Dakota referred to them as "Slota," meaning "Grease people," because of their custom of preserving dried bison meat and tallow in large rawhide bags called *taureaux*.

These métis buffalo hunters, who had met the Dakotas earlier in the day, were apparently on their guard when the Dakotas attacked their camp. They had corralled their horse- or ox-drawn carts in a circle around a big depression where their horses and other stock was kept. The métis had good long-range rifles and even a small cannon, with which they kept the Dakotas at a distance. The Dakotas could do little but long-range sniping, and the métis were very good at sniping back.

Many were killed on both sides in this fight. His-knife, a friend of White Bull, and a marksman, found that his gun had jammed and foolishly stood up to fix it. He was almost instantly shot in the forehead and killed. He rolled down the hill some distance and lay under the enemy's fire. White Bull jumped up and ran to His-knife, seized him by the right wrist, and dragged him over the hill. (Vestal, pp. 154–162)

PAGE 37 (*Plate 27*)   WHITE BULL RESCUES A WOUNDED
                        CHEYENNE

In this pictograph White Bull is shown rescuing another fallen comrade while under intensive fire from the enemy. He wears a tailed warbonnet in which alternating natural black and white and dyed red eagle feathers produce a colorful effect. The man being rescued has a curious war charm tied to his hair consisting of the stuffed skin of a water dog (salamander). These objects, or beaded buckskin replicas thereof, are common among the Cheyennes and Arapahos. A red spot on the man's abdomen marks the location of his wound. At the left are rows of hoofprints, indicating mounted warriors, a crude representation of a rifle, and many puffs of smoke, representing gunfire. Surrounding White Bull and his comrade are several streaks, representing flying bullets or balls, and a few more hoofprints, showing that this was the field of battle over which the fighting raged.

Pte san hunka le wicaton icu welo le Śahiyela ca wo rpape lo
owakiye cokan ake wana el iblamni na iwacu welo Śahiyela icante
waśte pelo kola oterike lo kolapila eyaś lena wookla ke lo ca bluha
yelo wanlakapelo kolapila akicize wanji el waon na hecamon helo
kola. Onjinjin tka wakpa etu okicize tanka etu welo oteri yelo
waniyetu 26 years etu welo kola. Akicitapi susuni kangi wicaśa
watakpe a u canke wicaśa ota rci okicize yelo mazakan kin lila uta
pelo le (Wihinapa) le cajeyelo Śahiyela kin hecetu kola.

This is White Bull recovering a body. This Cheyenne had been
shot down. I went right out in the middle of things again and got
him. The Cheyennes were very glad about this. It was very hard,
my friends, but I did it just as I have described it. Everything I tell
you is the truth, and you have seen that I did it, my friends. This
was a battle where I was right in the middle of the action, my
friend. It was on Rosebud Creek that this big battle took place. It
was a hard fight. I was twenty-six years old at the time, friend.
There were soldiers, Shoshonis, and Crows who came charging
us, and a lot of men were fighting. The gunfire was heavy. This
man was named Sunrise. He was a Cheyenne, my friend.

This rescue took place during the Battle of the Rosebud,
described by White Bull on page 23 of his account. The
Cheyenne, Sunrise, was shot through the belly from behind
and lay helpless. White Bull dismounted, ran forward under
fire, seized the Cheyenne by the wrists, and dragged him back
to safety. Sunrise died, however, shortly after they got him
back to camp. Because of the peculiar war charm the man
wore in his hair some of the Dakotas remember Sunrise as
"Water Dog." (Vestal, p. 189)

PAGE 38 (*Plate 28*)   WHITE BULL BRINGS BACK WHITE DEER

This pictograph is the last of the group which show
White Bull rescuing comrades-in-arms or recovering their
bodies from the field of battle. White Bull, dressed in a plain

buckskin shirt and blue cloth leggings, with a blanket belted around his waist, is carrying a wounded man dressed in a hooded green capote and leggings. The wounded man's arms are over White Bull's shoulders where White Bull has grasped the wrists. At the left a rectangular field of dots, labeled "Lena Lakotapi epelo" ("These are the Dakotas"), identifies the Sioux position. From this spot a dotted line extends to the right, bends in an arc, and ends at White Bull's feet, indicating the path he took in rescuing his friend. At the right we see two soldiers partially concealed in grass or brush, who are firing on the Indians.

> Pte san hunka le eca wicaton icu welo. Le (Tarca ska) eca wa onkapi eyaṡ onyan napapi ca ake el mni na kici waku welo maku-tepi eyaṡ ma opi ṡni yelo waniyetu ca waṡme lo oteri kelo Mniko-wojupi na Itazipcopelo ota pelo. Tiyata awakliyelo hehan waniyetu 26 years wani cokam yetu welo hecetu kolapila tanyan ecamon keyapelo karmi tanka etu welo.

> This is White Bull recovering a body. This was White Deer. They hit him but then they ran away, so again I went out there and we came back together. They shot at me but they didn't hit me. It was winter and there was deep snow which made it difficult to accomplish. There were a lot of Miniconjous and Sans Arcs there. I brought him home. I was twenty-six years old at the time. It was midwinter, my friend. They say I did a fine thing. This was at Big Bend.

PAGE 39 (*Plate 29*)   WHITE BULL STEALS CROW HORSES

This is the first of a series of pictographs in which White Bull records his horse-stealing exploits. Stealing horses from the enemy was highly regarded by the Dakotas, and consti- tuted a war honor. In this pictograph White Bull depicts himself running off a herd of horses (seven horses and two colts) from the vicinity of a Crow camp. Four of the adult horses are labeled *le waśte* ("this was a good one") and the two colts are labeled *cincala*, meaning "young ones." The two colts are drawn about one-fifth the size of the adult horses. At the far right is a drawing of the Crow camp, with hoofprints indicating the original position of the stolen horses. The camp is labeled *Kangi wicaśa lena ti pelo*, which may be translated "this is the Crow camp."

Chief White Bull Pte san hunka le e. Waniyetu lena makeca 24 years onkleklerapi śni tiyata onkli hunni pelo waśte yelo topa can el onkli hunni pelo lila onkupelo.
[The text at the upper left reads:]
Kinyukanpi cinca
Tatankinyotake tonskaku eyelo

Chief White Bull. I was twenty-four years old. We brought them home safely. It took us four days to get home. They were really chasing us.
[The text at the upper left may be translated:]
Son of Makes-room
Nephew of Sitting Bull

PAGE 40 (*Plate 30*) HORSES FROM THE CUSTER FIGHT

In this pictograph White Bull represents himself running off a herd of seven enemy horses. White Bull wears his *wotawe*, or war charm, and his own mount has a scalp attached to the bridle bit, indicating, in the Dakota system of heraldry, that this horse has been used to ride down an enemy.

[The Dakota text reads:] Pte san hunka e Chief White Bull. lena on ocaśtanpi heca yelo kola taku ecamon ki lena wanlakapelo wana kolapila wana len wahi omaka len wana waniyetu lena makeca yelo August 10 1931 81 years
[The text continues at the right as follows:] Waniyetu lena makeca etu welo 26 years. Pehin hanska ktepi na hi han na hehan

ake huta patan a u watakpe a u hetan ekta wa i na lena awica waku
kota a ye el wica yuha wakuca wanmayanka pelo kola kanġi
wicaśa ko a u welo kola

[The Dakota text may be translated:] This is Chief White Bull.
This was a great deed, my friend. Everyone took notice of what I
did on this occasion, friends. I have since come this far, August 10,
1931. I am now eighty-one years old.

[The text at the right may be translated:] At that time I was
twenty-six years old. It was at the time Long Hair was killed. The
next morning they were charging from downstream. I took part
in one charge and then I went and got these [horses] and was
bringing them back and they saw me, friend. Crow Indians were
coming, my friend.

PAGE 41 (*Plate 31*)   WHITE BULL'S FIRST BRAVE DEED

In this pictograph we see White Bull running off a herd of
eight horses from an enemy camp circle. White Bull, dressed
in a buckskin shirt and leggings and a long red breechcloth,
is armed with a bow and arrows. He is riding his horse Swift
Hawk, which also appears in pictographs 11, 12, and 13. This
horse was a dapple gray (Vestal, p. 40) but is colored blue in
these pictographs. The horse has a protective charm tied
around its neck.

[The principal Dakota text, which begins at the upper left of
the page, reads:] Pte san hunka le eyelo le tokeyelaŕci hecamon
welo kola waniyetu lena makeca etu welo 16 years len hecamon
welo kola Kola hiśa ki le onma (Tatankiyotake) wakakli yelo kola
owaton la yelo wiśkĕhan cantku yurla yeci etu welo kola le hunkpapa ya yelo le naronpa kola.

[The Dakota text at the upper right, near the camp circle
pictograph, reads:] Lena tokeca tipi eyaś takupi kin slonwayeśni
yelo lena etan ca iwica wacu welo onpahan reska ca el wicoti yelo.

[The Dakota text at the bottom of the page reads:] Kola wicaśa ota ai yelo he on narmala iblamina hecamun [*sic*] welo kola Mniko-wojupi etanhanpi Oglalapi etanhanpi Itazipco etanhanpelo he on waśte yelo. Natan a u canke om kicizapelo na toka ki etan wicakte pelo el ble śni yelo lena e e wica yuha waku ki he on hecetu welo kola.

[The principal Dakota text may be translated:] This is White Bull. This was the first noteworthy deed I accomplished, my friend. I was sixteen years old when I did this, my friend. Friend, one of the sorrel horses I gave to Sitting Bull. [The next phrases are not clear, and the meaning could not be supplied by any of my informants.] It was straight [?] teasing [?] breast striped [?] from these my friend. He was a Hunkpapa. Now you have heard it, my friend.

[The text at the upper right may be translated:] These are enemy tipis, but which tribe I do not know. From this camp I secured them. It was at dawn. The enemy camp was at White Mountain.

[The Dakota text at the bottom of the page reads:] My friend, a lot of men went on this war party. Stealthily I crept up and did the deed, my friend. There were members of the Miniconjou, Oglala, and Sans Arc subbands in the war party. It was a successful raid. They came charging out [from their camp] and we fought them. Some of the enemy were killed. I did not go out to fight as I was bringing my horses back, friend.

PAGE 42 (*Plate 32*)   STEALING HORSES AT WHITE MOUNTAIN

In this pictograph we again see White Bull running off a horse herd from an enemy camp. He is dressed as in the preceding pictograph, and is riding his dapple-grey pony Swift Hawk. White Bull is urging on the captured horses with his medicine lance, the lance given to him by his father at the same time he gave the boy Swift Hawk. Two of the captured ponies have saddles and bridles. The enemy camp is labeled *lecel wicoti ca etan*, meaning "this is the camp from which I took them."

Wana waniyetu lena makeca yelo 81 years 1931 August 10. Pte
san hunka Chief White Bull Wiyarpe yata Re ska wanihuku wicoti
etan lena owica wakli yelo waniyetu lena makeca hehan 16 years
etu lila wicaśa ota zuya a i ca narmala ibla mni na hecamon welo.
Ate (Kinyukanpi) lena a e con ki amakiyaka canke ecel ecamon
welo kola pila waśte yelo lila kola lena on ocaśtanpi ki heca yelo.
[The text at the upper right reads:]
    Kinyukanpi ate wayelo
    Tatankinyotake lekśi wayelo kola ho hecetu welo
    Śunkakan le lila luza helo okan make ci le hito ki le kola

I am now, August 10, 1931, eighty-one years old. Chief White
Bull. Over west below White Mountain there was an enemy camp.
From this camp I brought them [the horses] back. I was sixteen
years old at the time. There were many warriors on this expedition. I approached the camp stealthily and did the deed. My
father, Makes-room, praised me highly for this deed. My friends,
it was very good. My friend, it was a great deed.
[The text at the upper left may be translated:]
    Makes-room is my father.
    Sitting Bull is my uncle, friend.
That is the way it was. These horses were very fast. The horse I
am riding [in the picture] is a gray, my friend.

PAGE 43 (*Plate 33*)   WHITE BULL STEALS TWO PONIES

In this pictograph we see White Bull returning from a raiding expedition with two stolen animals. He wears his *wotawe*,
or war charm, and his mount is decorated with eagle feathers.

Pte san hunka Chief White Bull hel waniyetu lena makeca etu
26 years. Re ska waṇ el wicoti ca etan lena yus iwicawacu welo
wiyorpe yata wicaśa ota a i yelo naïma la iblamni woecun welo
lena on ocaśtanpi heca yelo kolapila wana len wahi waniyetu
81 years August 11, 1931.
[At the upper left the text reads:]

Kin yukanpi le cinca
Tatanka iyotake tonśkaku lekśi wa welo

This is White Bull. I was twenty-six years old at the time. There was an enemy camp at White Butte, and a great party had gone out west there on a raid. I stole up to the herd and accomplished this. It was a great deed and I was highly praised for it. My friends, I am now eighty-one years old, August 11, 1931

[The text at the upper left may be translated:] I am the son of Makes-room and the nephew of Sitting Bull, who is my uncle.

PAGE 44 (*Plate 34*) WHITE BULL STEALS A CROW HORSE
NORTH OF BEAR BUTTE

In this pictograph we see White Bull running off a horse from an enemy camp. White Bull is magnificently attired in a pink shirt, long red breechcloth, and beaded white leggings. On his chest he wears a *wawoslata wanapin*, or hair-pipe breastplate, and over his shoulder his *wotawe*, or war charm. A single eagle feather depends from his hair in back, and on the crown of his head is a small ring with a yellow eagle plume tied to it. His horse, a brown with white stockings, has a scalp attached to the bridle bit, indicating that the horse has been used to ride down an enemy. At the right of the pictograph is an enemy camp circle with hoofprints in it indicating the location of the enemy. Two lines of hoofprints connect the two horses, White Bull's mount and the stolen steed, with this camp. The small figure of a Crow Indian appears at lower right. This man is in the act of firing a rifle at the fleeing White Bull. A wavy line at the extreme right indicates that the Crow camp was on a river.

Pte san hunka e Mato paha iyececa i waziyata han wicoti wan etan le iwacu Lakota wikcemna 10 onkipi etanhan han awicaklipi. Kanǵi wicaśapi seca lila kuwa onka upelo om kicizapi econ qun

pelo hecetu waśte yelo waniyetu lena makeca etu 23 years len tu
wana len wahiyelo. 81 years 1931 August 11. len le a wawayelo ti
pi ki ikiyelo lila makute pelo.

This is White Bull. It was north of the Hill-like-a-bear [Bear
Butte] where there was an enemy camp. I took it from that camp.
There were ten of us Lakotas who went on this raid. They were
probably Crow Indians and they really chased us hard. We had a
running fight with them and got away. It was a successful raid.
I was twenty-three years old at the time. Now I have arrived at
the age of eighty-one, August 11, 1931. When we were close to the
camp they kept up a heavy fire.

PAGE 45 (*Plate 35*)   WHITE BULL AND A COMPANION RAID A
SMALL CAMP

In this pictograph White Bull is shown running off two
horses, a black and a brown, from a small enemy camp. He
rides a brown himself, and his mount is decorated with eagle
feathers tied in the mane and the tail. He wears a pink shirt
and blue cloth leggings and is armed with a carbine. The
enemy camp, apparently small, as only two tipis are shown,
is represented as being on a small creek which flows into a
larger stream.

Pte san hunka le eyelo. Ṙe ska wan el wicoti ca wanjila kicila
zuya wa i na lena yusloha i wica wacu welo hanhepi ehanl waśte
yelo kola hehan waniyetu lena makeca yelo 26 years wana len
wahi yelo omaka len 1931 August 11. Anpetu len ni wa on welo
kolapila.

This is Chief White Bull. At White Mountain there was an
enemy camp. I went on this raid with just one companion. I led
them [the stolen horses] back at night. It was good, friend. At that
time I was twenty-six years old. Now I am still alive and it is
August 11, 1931, my friends.

↑ Plate 29

↓ Plate 30

Plate 31

Plate 32

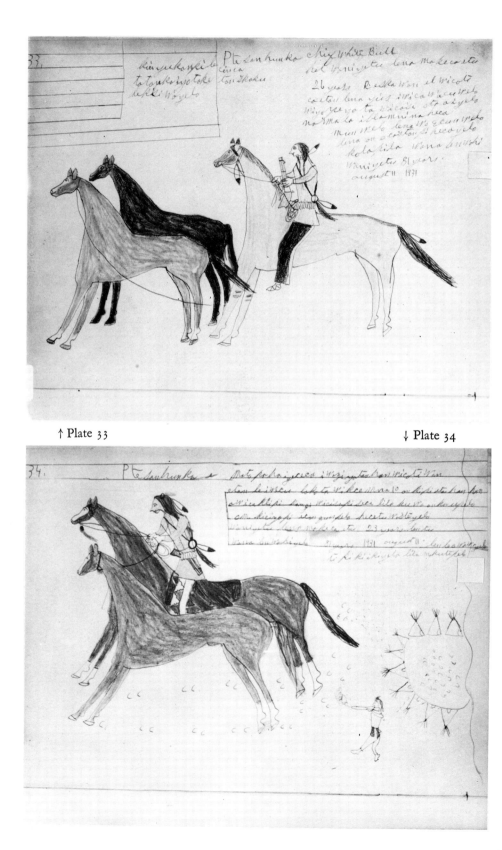

↑ Plate 33

↓ Plate 34

35. Pte sanknmka le eyela B eskovíin el nicoti ca wanjila kicila guya tti na lena yuastila wicawicu wela kankyi ekonl nictayela kola kolan wikiyela lena Maka sayela 21 years wanni len nikiyela aMakosku 1931 august 11. anleteu len ni wan an wilo kolapila

↑ Plate 35

26. Pte sanknmka chiy White Bull tatanka wanjila kicila wisina lena lila ota aWi enokliyela kehan Waniyetu lena Make coyela 26 years kecetn wela kola Wikce mna otapi tha wiksinya niyela aMaka Wanjila shel Wicorsn ota yela kola

↓ Plate 36

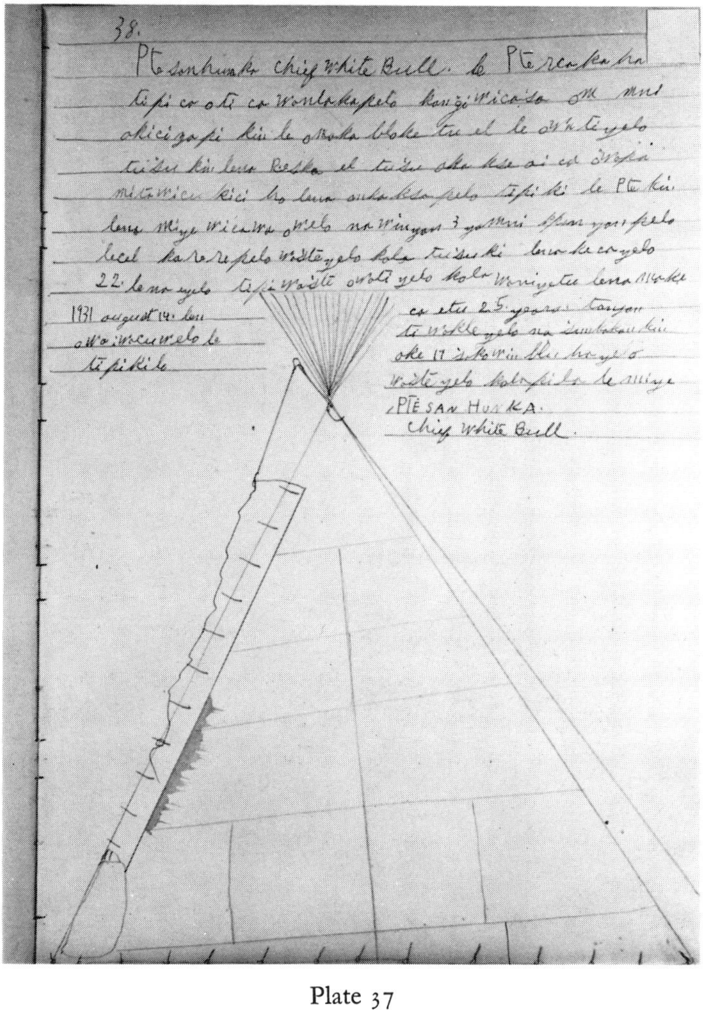

38.

Pteśanhunka chief White Bull. Le Pteśanhunka
tipi co oti ca Wonlakapelo kanzi wicaśa om mni
okicijapi kin le oyaka bloke tu el le White yelo
tiśu kin lena Reśla el tuśu oka kśe ai ca iśeyapi
mitawicu kici ho lena onlakloapelo tipi ki le Pte kin
lena miye wicakta yelo na Winyan 3 yamni oyanyanpelo
lecel kararupelo Waśteyelo Hola tuśuki lena Kecoyelo
22 lena yelo tipi Waśte oyata yelo Hola Woniyate lena Hoska

1931 august 14 lena
Woincuwelo le
tipi ki le

ca etu 25 years tanyan
ta Waśte yelo na iśmlalan kin
oke 17 iśko Win Blue howaye o
Waśteyelo Holapilo le miye
Ṕ PTE SAN HUNKA.
chief White Bull.

Plate 37

Plate 38

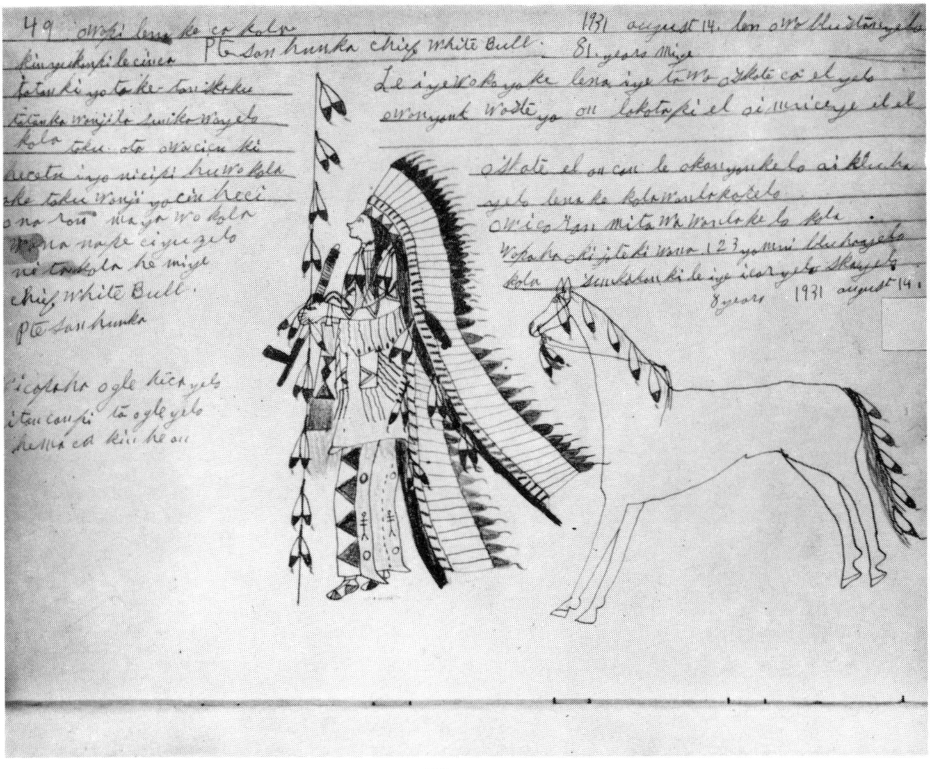
49
Pte San hunka chief White Bull.
1931 august 14.
81 years
chief White Bull.
Pte San hunka

Plate 39

PAGE 46 (*Plate 36*) WHITE BULL AND HIS BROTHER ONE
BULL STEAL HORSES

In this, the last of the horse-raid pictographs, we see White
Bull in the act of running off four horses from an enemy camp.
The camp, consisting of five tipis, is on a river or stream,
which is represented by a wavy line.

Pte san hunka Chief White Bull. Tatanka wanjila kicila wa i na
lena lila ota awicun kli pelo. Hehan waniyetu lena makeca yelo
26 years hecetu welo kola wikcemna otapi tka weksuye šni yelo
omaka wanjila el el owicoran ota yelo kola

Chief White Bull. I went with One Bull. We brought back many
this time. I was twenty-six years old at the time, my friend. There
were several tens[40] but I can't remember exactly how many. Within
that one season I performed many noteworthy deeds, my friend.

PAGE 47   SOME EVENTS OF WHITE BULL'S LATER LIFE

There is no pictograph on this page. The Dakota text reads:

Owicoran mitawa kin lena on Lakotapi el akicita   *1*. Imatancan
maqu pelo wicaša itancanpi heca maqu pelo.   *2*. Ate ohe okna na
hehanl wašicun la tan han tonkašila yapi tawicoȟan wawoyuspa
owapa   *3*. Nahehanl wayaco hemaca   *4*. Horwoju oyanke el lena
ehan na yelo na ake wawoyuspa hemaca   *5*. Na ake ake nupapi
eya onpi he mawanjin yelo   *6*. Oyate omniciye itancan hemaca
7. Ake iyapi awanyanka hemaca   *8*. Na hehanl wacekiye wicaša
hemaca   *9*. Na ake kaška itancan hemaca   *10*. Ake mayaska
owanyanka hemaca   *11*. Ake hunkayapi hemaca   *12*. Akicitapi
epi na Sapa wicaša om kicizapi kta ca el Tonkašila yapi ki el
yemašica ekta wa i na owicablu spelo   *13*. Na Horwoju el owi-
cawakli Sapa wicašapi kin hecetu ake Pehihanska rpa ye el a i ca

[40] The Dakotas use "tens" much as an English speaker uses "dozens."

owapa na el itancan maqu pelo *14*. Wašicun epi ca hecunpelo
akicita wowapi wan maqupi ake Rapid City el ośkate tanka el
oitcancan maqu pi yelo *15*. Ake Rapid City el Tonkašilapi wan
el i yunkan Řesapa ki mazaska ki mi šnala iwoglak ma šipi Lakotapi ki heyapi maqupi he on wowakla pelo canke hecetu keyelo
Tonkašila yapi ki eca anpetu letu le eyelo W.B. [this word is
unclear] Washington D.C., Oct. 31, 1911 letu welo.

[The second portion of the text reads:] Sapa wicaśa eya epeci
letu welo October 27, 1906. letan i blablelo na len owicablu spelo
Nov. 6, 1906. June 26, 1907 len awicawakliyelo July 4, 1907 wicoti
en naake Rapid City hektam okin inyanke wan el makiyutapi
3 yamni inyankapi ca mitawa wan el opa na tehanye rci wakapelo
okise oiyute mimela ca 6 šakpe yuhomnipi osni kiye šni letu Rapid
City July 3, 1904. Anpetu letu okanyanke ci ni on lehan Pierre,
South Dakota el akicita ohina Chief White Bull u wo eyapelo
wicaśa opawinge wanji 1000 wicayuha u wo eyelo Pehi hanska
okicize i lute kte lo eyelo iyecel ecamon welo kola a i yakapi yelo
wo ecun ki kola.

These are my deeds, recognized by the Dakota warriors: *1*. I was
made a chief. The men who were chiefs conferred this honor.
2. I followed the ways of my father and then I followed the ways
of the whites, as the President instructed us to do. Thus, I joined
the Indian Police. *3*. Since then I have served as tribal judge.
4. In the Miniconjou district some time ago I was also a policeman. *5*. There were twelve policemen there and I was one of
them. *6*. I was chairman of the tribal council. *7*. Another office
I held was that of sergeant-at-arms. *8*. I have also served as a
catechist. *9*. I also served as leader of the young men's [church]
group. *10*. I served a time as treasurer [of the church]. *11*. I
have also been a board member [of the church]. *12*. At the time
the Ute Indians were having difficulties and were going to fight
the soldiers, the government asked me to help so I went over
there and arrested them. *13*. I brought the Ute Indians back to
the Miniconjou district. I took part in the ceremonies at the place
where Long Hair fell, and they gave me a chieftainship. *14*. The
whites gave me a commission in the army. At a big celebration in
Rapid City I was made a chief. *15*. Another time in Rapid City
I conferred with the government officials concerning payment for

the Black Hills region. I was representing the entire Dakota tribe. The Dakotas asked me to speak for them and I did so at that time.

[The second portion of the text may be translated:] I learned the location of the Ute on October 27, 1906. I went where they were camped and arrested them on November 6, 1906. I brought them back on June 26, 1907. On July 4, 1907, there was an encampment in the hills back of Rapid City where a race meet was being held. A course three miles long had been laid out. I entered one of my own horses and it easily beat the others. The horse circled the half-mile track six times without stopping. This was at Rapid City July 3, 1904. The man who was [my] jockey that day is still alive and lives in Pierre, South Dakota.

Another time some military men came to me and said, "Chief White Bull, come and bring one thousand men with you. We want you to demonstrate how Custer and his command were killed." I did this and it was a beautiful re-enactment.

PAGE 48 LIFE AT THE AGENCY

Again there is no pictograph. The Dakota text reads:

Waniyetu 31 years lena makeca el wawoyuspa hemaca wa on oma 9 ka napciyunk ake wayacapi 3 yamnipi ca he ma wanji wani-yetu 4 tom na ake wawoyuspapi heca wa on waniyetu yamni 3 ake Ptekleśka opawinge wikcemna ake num awanwicayankpi el owapa wi śakpe 6 na ake iyecerci econpi ca owapa yelo 6 na Horwoju awakpamni el Lakotapi ki cincapi ki wayawapi kta ca micinca wanji makilapi ca wica wola na wowapi onspeyelo miye waniyetu lena makeca qun hehan yelo 30 years wana lena makeca yelo 30 years wana lena makeca yelo. Hokśila ca micinca ki le

George White Bull   55 years
Le cajeyelo

81 years   Little Eagel [sic]
1931 August 14   South Dakota

Wicoran mitawa oyaśila ociciyakelo kola.

When I was thirty-one years old I served as an Indian policeman. I was a policeman for nine years. I was also a judge, one of three selected. I served at this for four years. Then I was a policeman again for three years. I ran a herd of 1,012 cattle. I was employed in this way for six months, and then did another stint of six months. This was at the Miniconjou Agency. About this time they began sending the Dakota children to school. They asked me for one of my children and my son agreed to go and learn from books. I was thirty years old at the time and now I am eighty-one years old, August 14, 1931. My son, George White Bull as he is called, is fifty-five years old.

Little Eagle, South Dakota

I have now told you about all of my deeds, my friend.

PAGE 49 (*Plate 37*)   WHITE BULL'S TIPI

The pictograph on this page is merely a detailed side view of a Teton Dakota skin tipi. The drawing, though done with a ruler, is accurate, and minor details, such as the seams where the hides making up the cover are sewed together, are indicated.

Pte san hunka Chief White Bull. Le Pteřca ka ha tipi ca oti ca wanlaka pelo. Kanǧi wicaśa om mni akicizapi kin le omaka bloketu el owati yelo tu śu kin lena Ře ska el tu śu okakse a i ca owapa mitawicu kici ho lena onka ksa pelo tipi ki le Pte kin lena miye wicawa o welo na winyan 3 yamni kpan yan pelo lecel karere pelo waśte yelo kola tu śu ki lenakeca yelo 22 lena eyelo tipi waśte owati yelo kola waniyetu lena makeca etu 25 years. Tanyan ti wakle yelo na śunkakan kin ake 17 śakowin bluha yelo waśte yelo kolapila le miye   PTE SAN HUNKA

Chief White Bull

1931 August 14 len owa iwacu welo le tipi ki le

Chief White Bull. This is a picture of the buffalo-hide tipi in which I lived. I was living in it the summer they were fighting with the Crow Indians across a body of water. The poles you see we cut at White Mountain. I was with my wife cutting these

tipi poles. The buffalo I shot and three women tanned them. They were good seamstresses, my friend. For a good tipi of this sort twenty-two poles were required, friend. I was twenty-five years old at the time. I had a fine lodge and seventeen horses of my own. It was good, my friends. Chief White Bull.
I wrote this August 14, 1931

PAGE 50 (*Plate 38*)   THE CEREMONIAL CAMP CIRCLE OF THE
                        MINICONJOU

The pictograph is a representation of a Teton Dakota camp circle, specifically, that of the Miniconjou subband. Fifteen tipis are shown around the perimeter of the circle, and the sacred thunder tipi is in the center. Before the thunder tipi is a small fire over which a kettle is boiling, tended by a squatting figure. An erect figure, with outstretched hands stands nearby. Four other figures are shown around the edge of the circle, three walking figures and one seated figure smoking a pipe. Two of the walking figures also carry pipes and walking staves. Footprints lead from several of the tipis to the thunder tipi in the center. Between the tipis making up the circle are racks upon which meat is drying. The opening of the camp circle is to the left of the page (East).

Many elements in the pictograph are labeled in the Dakota language, for example, the dried meat at the top of the page is labeled *Talo wakablapelo—Talo welo watkeyelo*, which may be translated: "Meat which has been cut up and hung up to dry."

Several of the tipis in the camp circle are identified by owner. A red tipi at the left of the entrance is labeled *Pte san hunka le ti itancan*, "White Bull's tipi, he is a chief." A black and white tipi opposite the entrance is labeled *He wanjica le ti itancan*, "Chief One-horn's tipi." A red and white one at the right of the entrance is labeled *Itancan Kinya-hiyaye le ti*, which translates "Chief Comes-flying's tipi." A green and red one a bit farther on is labeled *Itancan Maraska le ti yelo*, "Chief White-swan's tipi."

The entrance to the camp circle is labeled *Le hunkpa eyapelo Lakotapi ki le caje yelo kola*, meaning "The Hunkpapas were named because they camped here [at the end of the circle] according to the Dakotas."

The tipi in the center of the camp circle is labeled *Kangi wakuwa le ti yelo le tipi yakihe el wicaśa ota el yakapelo wakinya tipi yelo*, which may be translated "This is Crow-hunter's lodge. He lived here. This was the band headquarters and many men sat there in council. It was the [sacred] thunder tipi."

The entire pictograph of the camp circle bears a central label reading: *Tipi ki lena lecel owapi ca otipi okitan inyan oti pelo kola*, which means "I have diagramed these tipis as I remember them from living in the camp, my friend."

[The principal Dakota text reads:] Ehanna rcelo Mnikowoju itancanpi lena lila oyate otapi tka le conala wakarelo. Wicaśa waśte ota yelo nakun kola len owabluśtan yelo le August 14, 1931. Kola miye lena nape on wakaje lo kola. Talo ota yelo kablapelo watkeci lena Pte rca ka talo welo

[A subsidiary text at the left reads:] Ehanni Mni ikiyelo wojupi na lila waicaŕa ca he on icaje pelo ehanna san oni lecel cajepi tka yelo tanyan waicar yapi ca icaje pelo kola ate omakiya kelo kola caje waśte pelo kola

[The principal Dakota text may be translated:] A long time ago there were many chiefs in the Miniconjou subband, but only a few are left. There were many good men among them, my friend. Now I have finished writing, August 14, 1931. I wrote this with my own hand, friend. They dried a lot of meat and hung it up. This was buffalo meat.

[The subsidiary text may be translated:] A long time ago these people planted their fields close to the water and raised good crops there. It was from this that they received their name [Mini-conjou]. They maintained themselves that way, by raising fine crops. From this they got their name. My father told me this my friend. They had a good reputation, friend.

PAGE 51 (*Plate 39*) WHITE BULL IN FULL DRESS

In this pictograph, which is on the last page on which White Bull has drawn or written, he represents himself in the full ceremonial costume of a Teton chief. He wears a full double-trailed warbonnet, a long scalp shirt, beaded buckskin leggings, and moccasins to match. In his right hand he carries a feathered war staff and in his left a catlinite pipe with a quill-worked stem. Behind him is a white horse, perhaps the symbol of the White Horse Riders society, a group made up entirely of chiefs. The horse has feathers braided into the mane and the tail. This pictograph undoubtedly represents the older White Bull, as he appeared at the time he was preparing his manuscript.

Owapi kin lenakeca kola Pte san hunka Chief White Bull. 1931, August 14 len owablustan yelo 81 years miye. Le iye wokayake lena iye tawa oskate ca el yelo owanyank waste ya on Lakotapi el oimniceye el el. Oskate el on can le akanyanke lo a i klu ha yelo lenake kola wanlakapelo owicoŕan mitawa wanlake lo kola wapaha okijate ki wana 123 yamni bluhayelo kola sunkakan ki le iye icaryelo skayelo 8 years 1931 August 14.
[The Dakota text at the upper left reads:]
    Kinyukanpi le cinca
    Tatankiyotake tonskaku
    Tatanka wanjila sunka wayelo
Kola taku ota owacicu ki hecetu iyanicipi hu wo kola ake taku wanji yacin heci onaran maya wo kola wana nape ciyuzelo nita kola he miye Chief White Bull Pte san hunka wicapaha ogle heca yelo itancanpi ta ogle yelo hemaca kin he on.

I prepared these pages my friend. Chief White Bull. I finished this on August 14, 1931. I am eighty-one years old. This is me in my costume which is worn on festive occasions. It looks fine when worn at the gatherings of the Lakotas. I wear this while riding in parades, and you have seen me wearing it, my friend. You have seen my deeds pictured. My warbonnet is double trailed. I have owned three of these, friend. The white horse I raised from a colt. It is eight years old August 14, 1931.

[The Dakota text at the upper left may be translated:]

I am the son of Makes-room.

I am the nephew of Sitting Bull.

One Bull is my brother.

My friend, I have written and given many things to you. Are you satisfied? If there is any other thing that you wish let me hear from you. Then, I shake hands with you. I am your friend, Chief White Bull. The shirt I am wearing is a scalp shirt. It is the shirt of a chief. I am one of them.

Bibliography

BOURKE, JOHN G. *On the Border with Crook*. Chicago: Rio Grande Press, 1962. Reprint of the 1891 edition.

DENSMORE, FRANCES. *Teton Sioux Music*. Bureau of American Ethnology Bulletin 61. Washington, 1918.

HOWARD, JAMES H. "The Cultural Position of the Dakota: A Reassessment." In *Essays in the Science of Culture in Honor of Leslie A. White*, ed. Gertrude E. Dole and Robert L. Carneiro (New York: Thomas Y. Crowell Co., 1960), pp. 249–268.

——. *Dakota Winter Counts as a Source of Plains History*. Anthropological Papers No. 61, Bureau of American Ethnology Bulletin 173. Washington, 1960. Pp. 335–416, pls. 45–47.

——. "Return from a Raid," *North Dakota Quarterly*, Vol. XXIX, No. 2 (Spring 1961), pp. i–ii.

——. "The White Bull Manuscript," *Plains Anthropologist,* Vol. VI, No. 12, Pt. 2 (1961), pp. 115–116.

MALLERY, GARRICK. *Pictographs of the North American Indians*. Fourth Annual Report of the Bureau of American Ethnology, 1882–1883. Washington, 1886.

——. *Picture Writing of the American Indians*. Tenth Annual Report of the Bureau of American Ethnology, 1888–1889. Washington, 1893.

RIGGS, STEPHEN R. *A Dakota-English Dictionary*. Ed. J. O. Dorsey. Contributions to North American Ethnology. Vol. VII: U.S. Geographical and Geological Survey of the Rocky Mountain Region. Washington, 1890.

SMITH, J. L. "A Short History of the Sacred Calf Pipe of the Teton Dakota," *Museum News* (the W. H. Over Dakota Museum), Vol. XXVIII, Nos. 7–8 (July–August 1967).

VESTAL, STANLEY. *Warpath: The True Story of the Fighting Sioux Told in a Biography of Chief White Bull.* Boston: Houghton Mifflin Co., 1934.

———. "The Man Who Killed Custer," *American Heritage*, Vol. VIII, No. 2 (February 1957), pp. 4–9, 90–91.

WILDSCHUT, WILLIAM. *Crow Indian Medicine Bundles.* Ed. John C. Ewers. Contributions from the Museum of the American Indian, Vol. XVIII. New York, 1966.

WISSLER, CLARK. *Societies and Ceremonial Associations in the Oglala Division of the Teton Dakota.* Anthropological Papers of the American Museum of Natural History, Vol. XI, Pt. 1. New York, 1912.